Legacy

The Good Kings of Judah

SAGE
WORDS

Pedro, Ohio

Legacy

The Good Kings of Judah

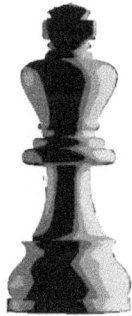

A TEXT MESSAGE STUDY
BY PAULA WISEMAN
STUDY THE TEXT • LIVE THE MESSAGE

Legacy: The Good Kings of Judah/Paula Wiseman. -1st ed. ISBN 978-0-9986505-5-5

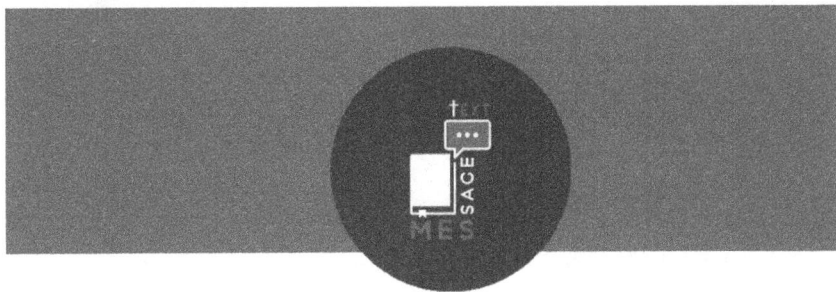

What is a Text Message Study?

Text messages have revolutionized how we communicate. They are instantly accessible. While we may not immediately respond, most of us will at least check the sender and even read the message.

The Bible is the ultimate TEXT because it comes from God Himself. God has chosen to reveal Himself to us. In the logo, the T is a cross. This is a reminder that God's revelation is a great redemption story accomplished by the work of Jesus Christ on the cross.

You'll notice there are THREE DOTS in the Bible's speech bubble. You've no doubt seen those when the person on the other end of the conversation is typing a message. In our logo, they remind us that God always has more to say to us. We will never exhaust His word.

If we become experts in the biblical text, though, and never put the things we learn into practice, we have failed. So the application, the MESSAGE, is a key part of getting into God's word.

Finally, STUDY implies that it takes a little effort. It's not skimming or scanning. But I guarantee it's worth it!

Paula

Jeremiah 29:13

Table of Contents

Legacy: The Good Kings of Judah

We know King David. And Solomon. Maybe even Hezekiah and Josiah. But there were many other kings in Judah, and admittedly, some were terrible.

However, there were some good kings, not perfect kings, but good kings. These good kings can serve as examples of things we can do, even in our culture, in our lives to honor God. And because they weren't perfect, they also serve as warnings to us. Over the next few weeks, we will look at some of them and glean what we can from their testimony.

This study is for you if. . .
- You ever wanted to do right but wavered.
- You ever looked to the wrong people for help.
- You ever walked away from God.
- You ever felt pressure to conform to the culture.
- You ever suffered great failures after great victories.
- You ever wondered if a godly life is worth it.

Maybe you're not into history, and people with unusual names make things confusing and hard to follow. But Paul assures us that all of the Old Testament is good to study. He even encouraged the Roman Christians to dig into the Scriptures.

> For whatever was written in former days was written for our instruction, that through endurance and through the encouragement of the Scriptures we might have hope. Romans 15:4

So all of these guys—Asa, Jehoshaphat, Joash, Amaziah, Uzziah, and Jotham—should encourage us and bring us hope. That's why we have their stories.

A note on Kings versus Chronicles

Let me address two questions right off the bat. *Why are there two accounts for these kings?* and *Why are the details different?*

Kings was written around the time of the fall of Judah. We don't know the actual author(s), but the books include example stories that often follow the official accounts, so it seems at the very least the author had access to the court records. The purpose is to relate to us the history of the kings of Israel and Judah, including whether or not they obeyed God.

All history is interpreted by the writer, so we need to keep in mind what the writer of Kings wanted us to understand. He shows us the gradual descent into idolatry that brought about God's judgment on the nation. Idolatry is serious business. God does not overlook it.

In the larger story of Scripture, the books of Kings show us exactly what Moses, and later Samuel, warned Israel about. Having a king rule over you will only lead to trouble. Israel failed under the judges and they fail under the kings. This points them to the arrival of the Messiah in the New Testament.

Chronicles was written after the Jews returned from seventy years of Babylonian captivity. The writer, Ezra perhaps, wanted to inform this returning generation about their heritage and about the God they served. 1 Chronicles generally follows 1 and 2 Samuel, while 2 Chronicles follows the books of Kings.

The writer of Chronicles focuses on Judah and often highlights the positive, celebrates the victories and works to instill in the people their identity as God's chosen nation. Worship and seeking the Lord are important themes in the book. This makes sense when you consider it was written at a time when the exiles were rebuilding the Temple and trying to re-establish worship.

In the big picture, Chronicles shows us that God's promise that a King, an eternal king, would come from David's line was not nullified because of the judgment and exile in Babylon. So we can take heart that our actions, our failures, our sins don't invalidate God's promises to us.

Paul reminded Timothy of this very thing.

> If we are faithless, He remains faithful; He cannot deny Himself. 2 Timothy 2:13 (NKJV)

The kings are people, and at their core, they are very much like us.

NOTE: The Scripture passages are taken from different translations. The reason for this is so that we focus on what the text says and not what we *remember* it saying. When the wording is just a little different, our brains engage. Engaging our brains and hearts to transform our lives is the goal of the study.

Asa–The Bold King

Prepare

Gather your study materials—Bible, notebook, pens, and pencils. Settle into your favorite study spot. Take a few moments to settle your heart and mind and detach from the concerns of your daily routine. You are preparing to enter the throne room of the King, and He has something to say to you. Make sure you are ready to hear it.

Open your study time with prayer. Ask the Holy Spirit to ensure you understand what God is saying. "Lord, the Apostle Paul said the things recorded in the Old Testament are there to teach us. Help me pay attention to the lessons You want me to learn. Help me do what is pleasing in Your sight."

♦   What does it mean to do what is right in the eyes of the LORD?

Text 1/3

1 Kings 15:9-15 (ESV)

9 In the twentieth year of Jeroboam king of Israel, Asa began to reign over Judah,

10 and he reigned forty-one years in Jerusalem. His mother's name was Maacah the daughter of Abishalom.

11 And Asa did what was right in the eyes of the LORD, as David his father had done.

12 He put away the male cult prostitutes out of the land and removed all the idols that his fathers had made.

13 He also removed Maacah his mother from being queen mother because she had made an abominable image for Asherah. And Asa cut down her image and burned it at the brook Kidron.

14 But the high places were not taken away. Nevertheless, the heart of Asa was wholly true to the LORD all his days.

15 And he brought into the house of the LORD the sacred gifts of his father and his own sacred gifts, silver, and gold, and vessels.

Study the Text

FOCUS

Take a few moments to FOCUS on the passage above. *(Since this is the first one, I'll give some hints.)*

What FACTS are presented? *(This passage is fact-heavy. It includes specifics about Asa's reign and some key reforms. Re-writing them helps you remember them.)*

Are there any instructions to OBEY? *(Not directly, but Asa did what was right by getting rid of idol worship. Don't worship idols goes all the way back to the Ten Commandments.)*

Do you see anything in the passage that reminds you of CHRIST? *(John 8:29—Jesus always did the things that please the Father. Also, He cleaned out the Temple twice because the worship did not honor God.)*

Was there anything that was difficult to UNDERSTAND? *(The passage is straightforward. However, there are some cultural/historical details that may be unfamiliar.)*

Are there any SINS to avoid? *(Idolatry.)*

Insights

9 twentieth year of Jereboam—A generation before this, Jereboam led the rebellion against Rehoboam that resulted in the divided kingdom. He established idol worship in the Northern Kingdom and will be held up as the epitome of evil and rebellion against God. Until Ahab, that is. It's his twentieth year, so it's not been that long since the split. Asa's dates are around 911-870 BC. He takes the reins at a time when Judah is still figuring out how the divided kingdom works.

♦ How essential is godly leadership when it comes to establishing the foundation for the future?

10 His mother's name was Maacah the daughter of Abishalom—Here's a situation where we need some critical thinking. Verse 2 of this same chapter lists Maacah as Abijam/Abijah's mother. That makes her Asa's grandmother. Verse 9 is more likely referring to her as the queen mother, her office rather than the relationship to Asa. Now, this is significant because Abishalom is a variant spelling of Absalom, the son of David, who led a coup against his father. 2 Chronicles 11:20-22 lists her as Rehoboam's favorite wife, so her son, Abijah, became the crown prince. Regardless of which generation she belonged to, she brings a heritage of idolatry and rebellion into the royal line. It's not unreasonable to assume she had some influence on the young prince Asa in his formative years. His later commitment to live a God-honoring life breaks away from that tradition.

♦ It is a very hard thing to have to choose between your family and your commitment to God. Say a prayer for the kids and teens in your neighborhood or in your church who are trying to live a God-honoring life but don't have support at home.

11 Asa did what was right—We will see in the next session that Asa has a significant failure in his walk with God. Notice the grace, though. His failures are not rehashed here. There is no qualifier or disclaimer. He did what was right. We would do well to remember that when we hear the whispers of the enemy who reminds us of our failures.

11 In the eyes of the LORD—This is the only standard that matters.

- What are some false standards we use to measure ourselves or our leaders?

11 As David his father—Of course, David was not Asa's biological father. He was Asa's ancestor. This is a figure of speech. But it is very high praise for Asa. Only Hezekiah and Josiah are held in higher regard than Asa was. Connecting Asa to David is a commendation of his honoring God and his building the kingdom of Judah.

- How important is it to have godly examples in the past?

12-15 There are at least five important reforms that Asa accomplishes. List them below. Compare them to Moses's instructions in Deuteronomy 12:1-4

1.

2.

3.

4.

5.

- Are there any reforms on that list that may have been more difficult?

- Verse 14 begins with the word "But." Why do you think God inspired the writer to leave this shortcoming in the narrative?

- How do you reconcile that with the statement that Asa served

God wholeheartedly, that his heart was wholly true to the Lord?

Live the Message

Confronting and dealing with sin in our life is a difficult, messy business, especially when we start uncovering and tearing down the idols we hold on to. We need that same resolve, no matter where we find the idols, no matter how cherished they are. Let Asa be your example and boldly tear them from your life.

- ♦ Ask for God's help in identifying the idols you have in your heart. Then ask for His help in getting rid of them.

The whole reason for studying the Bible is to be transformed by what we learn about God and ourselves. Review the passage and your notes. What did you learn? How do those lessons speak to your life? Record them here. Also check pages 103-105.

(Don't overthink this, but if you are having trouble, here's an example to get you started: *When the Bible says Asa was wholly true to the LORD even though he left the high places, that gives me encouragement when I feel like I let God down. I am not perfect, but He sees my heart and knows my motivations.*)

> There's more to Asa's story in 2 Chronicles. I highly recommend reading and studying these texts. If you are using this study in a small group setting, you can opt to use them for additional sessions or for personal study in between meetings.

Text 2/3

2 Chronicles 14: 9-13 (ESV)

9 Zerah the Ethiopian came out against them with an army of a million men and 300 chariots, and came as far as Mareshah.

10 And Asa went out to meet him, and they drew up their lines of battle in the Valley of Zephathah at Mareshah.

11 And Asa cried to the LORD his God, "O LORD, there is none like you to help, between the mighty and the weak. Help us, O LORD our God, for we rely on you, and in your name we have come against this multitude. O LORD, you are our God; let not man prevail against you."

12 So the LORD defeated the Ethiopians before Asa and before Judah, and the Ethiopians fled.

13 Asa and the people who were with him pursued them as far as Gerar, and the Ethiopians fell until none remained alive, for they were broken before the LORD and his army. The men of Judah carried away very much spoil.

Study the Text

FOCUS

What FACTS are presented?

Are there any instructions to OBEY?

Do you see anything in the passage that reminds you of CHRIST?

Was there anything that was difficult to UNDERSTAND?

Are there any SINS to avoid?

Insights

9 Then—If you glance back at verses 6-8, you'll see Asa had just built a series of forts and strengthened the defenses of his cities. The army grew from the 40,000 troops his father had. Things were in pretty good shape. That's when the test came. Where will Asa place his faith?

9 Zerah the Ethiopian—Ethiopia was a powerful kingdom. Some historians and scholars believe Zerah may have been acting as a proxy for Egypt. His 300 chariots may not sound like much, but they gave an army an advantage comparable to the advantage tanks give. Remember how afraid the Israelites were of the Egyptian chariots that pursued them as they left Egypt (Exodus 14:9-10)? Verse 8 says Asa had a combined army of 300,000 foot soldiers and 280,000 arches, but no chariots. This left him outnumbered almost 2:1.

11 What were Asa's requests?

What does he say about God?

On what basis does Asa make his requests? (Hint: Look at the word "for." It answers the question "why.")

♦ How does our understanding of God's character influence how (or how often) we pray?

♦ What is our basis for approaching God in prayer? How do Hebrews 4:15-16, Hebrews 7:25, and Romans 8:34 apply?

13

12-13 What are the results of the battle?

Notice verse 13 says, "The Cushites fell until they had no survivors." This was an army of one million soldiers. Wiped out. The defeat is so devastating that we don't hear much out of Egypt on the world stage for another 150 years.

- ♦ Consider the implications of such a total victory, especially in light of Asa's prayer.

- ♦ Read 2 Chronicles 6:34. How are Asa's actions a fulfillment of Solomon's prayer?

- ♦ The Chronicler often highlights the military victories of Judah's past. How important is this for the nation of returning exiles? How important is it for us to remember our past victories?

If you looked at verses 6-8, you probably noticed that seeking the Lord was mentioned several times. This is another thread that runs through the narrative. (It's one of the key themes in Chronicles. Watch for it in later readings.)

Live the Message

It seems that any time we make progress or make a commitment to God, that commitment is tested. Asa immediately went to God in humility to ask for help. Think about the tests you currently face. Have you sought God's help?

♦ How likely are you to try and battle for a while by yourself before you ask for help? Why do you think that is?

Text 3/3

2 Chronicles 15:1-15

1 The Spirit of God came upon Azariah the son of Oded,

2 and he went out to meet Asa and said to him, "Hear me, Asa, and all Judah and Benjamin: The LORD is with you while you are with him. If you seek him, he will be found by you, but if you forsake him, he will forsake you.

3 For a long time Israel was without the true God, and without a teaching priest and without law,

4 but when in their distress they turned to the LORD, the God of Israel, and sought him, he was found by them.

5 In those times there was no peace to him who went out or to him who came in, for great disturbances afflicted all the inhabitants of the lands.

6 They were broken in pieces. Nation was crushed by nation and city by city, for God troubled them with every sort of distress.

7 But you, take courage! Do not let your hands be weak, for your work shall be rewarded."

8 As soon as Asa heard these words, the prophecy of Azariah the son of Oded, he took courage and put away the detestable idols from all the land of Judah and Benjamin and from the cities that he had taken in the hill country of Ephraim, and he repaired the altar of the LORD that was in front of the vestibule of the house of the LORD.

9 And he gathered all Judah and Benjamin, and those from Ephraim, Manasseh, and Simeon who were residing with them, for great numbers had deserted to him from Israel when they saw that the LORD his God was with him.

10 They were gathered at Jerusalem in the third month of the fifteenth year of the reign of Asa.

11 They sacrificed to the LORD on that day from the spoil that they had brought 700 oxen and 7,000 sheep.

12 And they entered into a covenant to seek the LORD, the God of their fathers, with all their heart and with all their soul,

13 but that whoever would not seek the LORD, the God of Israel, should be put to death, whether young or old, man or woman.

14 They swore an oath to the LORD with a loud voice and with shouting and with trumpets and with horns.

15 And all Judah rejoiced over the oath, for they had sworn with all their heart and had sought him with their whole desire, and he was found by them, and the LORD gave them rest all around.

Study the Text

FOCUS

What FACTS are presented?

Are there any instructions to OBEY?

Do you see anything in the passage that reminds you of CHRIST?

Was there anything that was difficult to UNDERSTAND?

Are there any SINS to avoid?

INSIGHT

1 **The Spirit of God**—After the victory, God has a message for His people.

♦ Are we as anxious to hear from God when things go WELL as we are when things are falling apart?

In verse 3, there are three things listed that Israel has been missing for many years.

1.

2.

3.

7 **Take courage. . . Don't let your hands be weak (don't give up)**—There is a sense that Azariah is encouraging Asa to build on this victory and not let history—the history in which they abandoned God and embraced idols—repeat itself.

♦ What victories—even past ones—can you build on?

7 **your work**—Based on verse 8, what work is Azariah, the prophet, likely referring to?

10 Third month, fifteenth year (May/June 897 BC)—According to the Hebrew calendar, this was the time the Feast of Weeks was celebrated. You can read about it in Leviticus 23:15-22. It commemorated the giving of the Law, fifty days after Israel left Egypt. In the New Testament, it is called Pentecost since it was celebrated fifty days after Passover. In Acts, the Holy Spirit empowers believers to carry out the gospel. What happens on this Pentecost?

12 they entered into a covenant—In Exodus, after the golden calf, Israel renewed their covenant with God. (Exodus 34:10-11ff). How does this connect with Asa's celebration?

♦   Is it worthwhile to renew our commitment to God from time to time? Does your commitment need renewing?

15 the LORD gave them rest all around—Rest and peace for the nation are a reflection of being in a right relationship with God. Skirmishes happen, but the era was marked by peace. Verse 19 says there was no war until the thirty-fifth year of Asa's reign. Those events are in the next session.

Count the number of times seeking God is mentioned in this passage._____

What happens when we seek God?

What happens if we don't seek Him?

Go to pages *** and add any new insights from these extra texts about Asa.

Live the Message

It is a fact of modern life that everything must be measured, counted, graphed, and analyzed, even things like church attendance, baptisms, and so forth. While numbers aren't bad, assigning too much worth to them can be. Asa's victory proves that superior numbers are not necessarily the indicator of success.

♦ Why do you think we place so much emphasis on numbers or other metrics?

♦ How can metrics be used for good?

♦ Read 1 Corinthians 3:5-10. What do those verses tell you about numbers in the kingdom?

Asa's Legacy

Asa boldly undertook reforms in his nation to bring them back to God-honoring living and worship. It didn't matter that his own grandmother was prominent in the idol-worshiping movement. His commitment to God was stronger, ran deeper than even his commitment to his family.

It's not likely that any of us will be in a position of power like Asa, but we do have the authority to make changes in our own lives. Have we allowed idolatry—attitudes or practices that draw our loyalty away from God—to seep in? Is career advancement our highest priority at the expense of holiness? Is building a following a more urgent goal than being a follower? Is fitting in with the culture more important than our commitment to Christ?

Asa also demonstrated bold leadership in pursuing God. In the fifteenth year of his reign, Asa saw the fruit of his commitment as the entire nation reaffirmed their covenant relationship with God alone.

In the same way, our pursuit of holiness can motivate others. We don't have to wait for our leaders or more mature Christians to make the first move. We can make that commitment today.

Our legacy won't just magically appear one day when we grow old. We are building it right now. What will you change tomorrow to ensure your legacy is a godly one? Record it below then pray and ask God to honor that commitment and help you keep it.

The whole reason for studying the Bible is to be transformed by what we learn about God and ourselves. Review the passage and your notes. What did you learn? How do those lessons speak to your life? Record them here. Also check pages 103-105.

Next Session

Asa experienced an incredible victory. It is easy to read his story and think, "If God intervened in my life like that, there's no way my faith would waver ever again!"

Asa, however, is all too human. The fact is all of us have woefully short memories and breathtaking self-centeredness. In the next session, we'll see how that plays out in Asa's life.

Asa—The Disappointing King

Prepare

Gather your study materials—Bible, notebook, pens, and pencils. Settle into your favorite study spot. Review your notes on Asa from the last session. Things are going to change drastically for the king. As we approach this session, keep in mind Paul's warning to the Corinthians.

> If you think you are standing strong, be careful not to fall. 1 Corinthians 10:12 (NLT)

Open your study time with prayer. Ask the Holy Spirit to help you approach the study with humility. "Lord, it is easy to look at someone else's failures with judgment. Help me to examine my own heart in the light of Your word."

- ♦ Does it matter who you partner with in business? In politics? In your personal life?

Text 1/2

1 Kings 15:16-24 (HCSB)

> 16 There was war between Asa and Baasha king of Israel throughout their reigns.

> 17 Israel's King Baasha went to war against Judah. He built Ramah in order to deny anyone access to Judah's King Asa.

> 18 So Asa withdrew all the silver and gold that remained in the treasuries of the LORD's temple and the treasuries of the royal palace and put it into the hands of his servants. Then King Asa sent them to Ben-hadad son of Tabrimmon son of Hezion king of Aram who lived in Damascus, saying,

19 "There is a treaty between me and you, between my father and your father. Look, I have sent you a gift of silver and gold. Go and break your treaty with Baasha king of Israel so that he will withdraw from me."

20 Ben-hadad listened to King Asa and sent the commanders of his armies against the cities of Israel. He attacked Ijon, Dan, Abel-beth-maacah, all Chinnereth, and the whole land of Naphtali.

21 When Baasha heard about it, he quit building Ramah and stayed in Tirzah.

22 Then King Asa gave a command to everyone without exception in Judah, and they carried away the stones of Ramah and the timbers Baasha had built it with. Then King Asa built Geba of Benjamin and Mizpah with them.

23 The rest of all the events of Asa's reign, along with all his might, all his accomplishments, and the cities he built, are written in the Historical Record of Judah's Kings. But in his old age he developed a disease in his feet.

24 Then Asa rested with his fathers and was buried in the city of his ancestor David. His son Jehoshaphat became king in his place.

Study the Text

FOCUS

FOCUS on the passage above. What FACTS are presented?

Are there any instructions to OBEY?

Do you see anything in the passage that reminds you of CHRIST?

Was there anything that was difficult to UNDERSTAND?

Are there any SINS to avoid?

Insights

16 Baasha, king of Israel—He had assassinated Jereboam's son and then murdered all of Jereboam's relatives (See 1 Kings 15:25-29. The accounts of the kings of Judah and Israel jump back and forth between kingdoms, so they aren't strictly chronological.) The northern kingdom of Israel had enjoyed peace for about a decade until Baasha seized the throne.

- ♦ No one is beyond reach of the gospel. Our compassion for people can't blind us to reality. Jesus was very frank with the woman at the well. He had sharp words for the Pharisees. He had no illusions about Herod. However, He genuinely grieved for those who would not hear His message. Think of a person or group you would consider an enemy of the gospel. Commit to pray for them. Ask God to help you see them with His eyes.

17 He built Ramah in order to deny anyone access to Judah's King Asa—Baasha put up a blockade. This is an act of war even today. From what we know of his character, he is not bluffing.

18 Asa withdrew all the silver and gold that remained in the treasuries of the LORD's temple and the treasuries of the royal palace and . . . sent them to Ben-hadad . . . king of Aram.—This is stunning. King Asa, who twenty years before defeated an army of one million Ethiopians, cleans out the Temple treasury and the royal treasury—ALL the silver and gold—and sends it to the King of Aram (Syria).

- ♦ What kinds of events would make us desperate enough to give up everything we owned? What emotions fuel that kind of desperation?

♦ Read 2 Chronicles 15:18. Some of the gold and silver was added to the Temple treasury by Asa. It is possible he thought he had a say in what happened to the treasure since he had donated it. Is this legitimate? What does it mean to consecrate a gift?

19 "There is a treaty between me and you . . . Go and break your treaty with Baasha king of Israel . . ."—And it gets worse. Asa entices Ben-hadad to go back on his word to Baasha. Now we know Baasha is rotten and question why anyone would want to align themselves with him. But for a man with a testimony and history of commitment to God to act in such a dishonorable way is hard to figure.

♦ We can speculate, but it is impossible to know the heart of another. When someone, especially a leader, folds during a crisis of faith, what impact does it have on the rest of the body? How should we respond afterward?

20 Ben-hadad listened to King Asa—Of course he did. This was a win-win for him. Not only did he get a sizable fortune, but he had access to the trade routes to the Mediterranean and to the Jezreel Valley. Judah has not heard the last of the Syrians. They will be back.

♦ Who benefits when we abandon our faith? Read 2 Samuel 12:13-14.

23 a disease in his feet—Ironically, the king's name means "God heals." Perhaps the illness had an additional symbolic meaning. Asa's problem was in his walk with God. Perhaps God was sending the king a message—if you won't stand firm in your commitment to me, you won't stand at all.

♦ Are there other ways in which our physical life reflects our spiritual life?

Live the Message

Who we turn to when things get difficult reveals who our faith is in. Regardless of what we profess, our actions unmask our hearts. We don't have a record of what might have prompted Asa to depart from his strong faith. Maybe some tragedy struck, the loss of a wife or a child. Who knows.

We also have an enemy who constantly works to make ineffective servants and witnesses for Christ. Read 1 Peter 5:6-10. What steps does he list that might protect us from the temptation to abandon our faith?

Which steps can you implement right now?

Verse 10 is a prayer Peter offers for his readers. Who can you enlist to pray for you? Who can you pray for? Record the names and dates.

In the account in 2 Chronicles 16, we get additional details about this episode in Asa's life. The additional study picks up after Baasha's army retreated, and Asa fortifies some frontier towns to prevent Baasha from threatening him again.

Text 2/2

2 Chronicles 16:7-14 (HCSB)

7 At that time, Hanani the seer came to King Asa of Judah and said to him, "Because you depended on the king of Aram and have not

depended on the LORD your God, the army of the king of Aram has escaped from your hand.

8 Were not the Cushites and Libyans a vast army with many chariots and horsemen? When you depended on Yahweh, He handed them over to you.

9 For the eyes of Yahweh roam throughout the earth to show Himself strong for those whose hearts are completely His. You have been foolish in this matter. Therefore, you will have wars from now on."

10 Asa was angry with the seer and put him in prison because of his anger over this. And Asa mistreated some of the people at that time.

11 Note that the events of Asa's reign, from beginning to end, are written in the Book of the Kings of Judah and Israel.

12 In the thirty-ninth year of his reign, Asa developed a disease in his feet, and his disease became increasingly severe. Yet even in his disease he didn't seek the LORD but only the physicians.

13 Asa died in the forty-first year of his reign and rested with his fathers.

14 He was buried in his own tomb that he had made for himself in the city of David. They laid him out in a coffin that was full of spices and various mixtures of prepared ointments; then they made a great fire in his honor.

Study the Text

FOCUS

FOCUS on the passage above. What FACTS are presented?

Are there any instructions to OBEY?

Do you see anything in the passage that reminds you of CHRIST?

Was there anything that was difficult to UNDERSTAND?

Are there any SINS to avoid?

Insights

7 Hanani the seer—A prophet of God.

7 "you depended on the king of Aram and have not depended on the LORD your God"—Without a 24-hour news cycle, it's hard to know how many of the people knew about the deal/bribe Asa had arranged. God knew, and so His prophet knew as well. Depended means "put your faith in." It is the same Hebrew word *shaan* used in 2 Chronicles 14:11 when Asa cried out to God when the Ethiopians came against him. Asa knew exactly what it was to rely on God. In verse 8, the prophet reminds him.

The old commentator Matthew Henry says Asa acted contrary to his experience, his knowledge, and his own best interest.

♦ This was not the last time Judah sought help from someone other than the LORD. Isaiah 30:1 delivers a stern warning against it. Knowing these things, we still turn to others for help. Why do you think that is?

9 For the eyes of Yahweh roam throughout the earth to show Himself strong for those whose hearts are completely His.—This is an amazing declaration. Think about that. God is actively looking for opportunities to intervene, to show Himself strong on behalf of those who are His. Asa missed out on this.

♦ Do we miss out on the opportunity for God to intervene because we don't demonstrate loyalty to Him? It is a sobering question. Are we courageous enough to ask God to show us where disloyalty lives in our hearts? Are we resolved enough to root it out?

9 "You have been foolish in this matter."—Throughout the book of Proverbs, foolishness is equated with a cynical rejection of God. Hanani accuses Asa of behaving like someone who doesn't believe in God.

- ♦ Do we ever act like someone who doesn't know God? Who has no Father? No Savior? No indwelling Holy Spirit? What does that look like? Does the rest of the world recognize it when we are disloyal to God?

9 "Therefore, you will have wars from now on"—By comparing accounts, we know that this is the thirty-fifth year of Asa's forty-one-year reign. Except for the incursion by the Ethiopians, Judah had enjoyed peace. Peace, rest in the land was a reflection of God's favor. That is being withdrawn. Review 2 Chronicles 15:2.

- ♦ Is it unreasonable for God to expect us to live according to His laws? What basis does He have? Do Revelation 4:11 and 5:9-10 offer any reasons?

10 Asa was angry with the seer and put him in prison—I have heard that the first thing you should do if you realize you are in a hole is to stop digging. Compare Asa's reaction here with David's reaction in 2 Samuel 12:13 and Psalm 51.

- ♦ Why is it so difficult to confess and repent when confronted with our sin?

10 And Asa mistreated some of the people at that time—Reading between the lines, I suspect Asa was mistreating or oppressing anyone who agreed with Hanani, that is, who thought the alliance with Syria was a bad idea. A political leader harassing someone who calls him out is as familiar to us as this morning's headlines.

- ♦ Before we come down too hard on Asa, how do we respond when our sins are brought to light? Do we call others narrow or unloving? Maybe sanctimonious and self-righteous? Do we dig in? Do we rally others to our side? How do you personally respond?

12 Yet even in his disease he didn't seek the LORD but only the physicians.—This is NOT an admonition against going to the doctor or taking advantage of the tremendous knowledge and advancements modern medicine has to its credit. It is not even a condemnation of Asa seeking medical treatment for a medical condition. The issue is that Asa, in his pride and stubbornness, refused to recognize that there was a spiritual dimension to this physical condition. Not every sickness is a direct result of our personal sin. We live in a fallen world, and one of the horrible effects of sin is that innocent people are hurt. In John 9:2-3, Jesus adds to the discussion that sometimes illness comes so that the works of God can be displayed in the sufferer's life. Additionally, there is speculation that the "physicians" Asa consulted were more on the order of witch doctors or voodoo practitioners, clearly violating the Law of Moses.

- ♦ Read Luke 10:34, 1 Timothy 5:23, and James 5:13-14. What is the relationship between medical remedy and prayer?

Live the Message

What does it say to the rest of the world when the people of God don't live according to the word of God? Following God, following Jesus Christ cannot be a temporary commitment. We can't sign on for a season or two and then lose interest. James says some pointed things about this.

Read James 1:2-8. What does he mean when he says "double-minded"?

How does being double-minded affect our witness?

Asa's Legacy

Amazing victories. Shocking failures. Sound familiar? More than we'd like to admit. As followers of Christ, we have the responsibility to work under the Holy Spirit's guidance to become more like Christ every day. At some point, Asa stopped trying. That's tragic enough in the life of any believer, but when it happens with a high-profile leader, it's even more painful. In recent months, we've seen famous professors of Christ renounce their faith and walk away. What should we think?
Remember, in God's grace, He still had His inspired writers record that Asa served the LORD wholeheartedly.

Asa was human. He had great success and failures. He is counted among one of the great kings of Israel. 2 Chronicles 16:14 tells us the people made a great fire in his honor when he died. They remembered his successes more than his failures. Listing him as a man who followed God with his whole heart shows that God remembered him that way too.
Asa doesn't teach us that it's no big deal to abandon our faith. On the contrary, there were lasting consequences for him and his kingdom because of his unwise decisions. Neither does Asa teach us that what God is looking for is 51%, just more good than bad.
What he teaches us is "the eyes of Yahweh roam throughout the earth to show Himself strong for those whose hearts are completely His." Don't be foolish in the matters of our life.

The whole reason for studying the Bible is to be transformed by what we learn about God and ourselves. Review the passage and your notes. What did you learn? How do those lessons speak to your life? Record them here. Also check pages 103-105.

Next Session

Asa had a son named Jehoshaphat, who was watching and taking notes. Because of his father's long reign, Jehoshaphat was thirty-five when he took the throne.

In the next session, we'll see that steadfast faith was not what Jehoshaphat struggled with.

Jehoshaphat—The Naïve King

Prepare

Gather your study materials—Bible, notebook, pens, and pencils. Settle into your favorite study spot. Consider Jesus's words in Matthew 10:16, "Behold, I send you out as sheep in the midst of wolves. Therefore be wise as serpents and harmless as doves." Matthew 10:16 (NKJV)

Open your study time with prayer. Ask the Holy Spirit to help you approach the study with wisdom and discernment.

♦   Do we have enemies as believers?

1 Kings 22:41-50 (NASB)

41 Now Jehoshaphat the son of Asa became king over Judah in the fourth year of Ahab king of Israel.

42 Jehoshaphat was thirty-five years old when he became king, and he reigned twenty-five years in Jerusalem. And his mother's name was Azubah the daughter of Shilhi.

43 He walked in all the way of Asa his father; he did not turn aside from it, doing right in the sight of the LORD. However, the high places were not taken away; the people still sacrificed and burnt incense on the high places.

44 Jehoshaphat also made peace with the king of Israel.

45 Now the rest of the acts of Jehoshaphat, and his might which he showed and how he warred, are they not written in the Book of the Chronicles of the Kings of Judah?

46 The remnant of the sodomites who remained in the days of his father Asa, he expelled from the land.

47 Now there was no king in Edom; a deputy was king.

48 Jehoshaphat made ships of Tarshish to go to Ophir for gold, but they did not go for the ships were broken at Ezion-geber.

49 Then Ahaziah the son of Ahab said to Jehoshaphat, "Let my servants go with your servants in the ships." But Jehoshaphat was not willing.

50 And Jehoshaphat slept with his fathers and was buried with his fathers in the city of his father David, and Jehoram his son became king in his place.

We're going to do things a little differently on this one. Jehoshaphat gets very light treatment from the writer of Kings. Because of that, we are going to focus on the Chronicles account for our study. However, this passage in 1 Kings gives us a good overview and outline for what's coming next.

---

43 he did not turn aside from it—In contrast to his father Asa, Jehoshaphat did not waver in his faith later in life.

In the middle of verse 43, we find the word **however** (or nevertheless, or yet, or something similar). Jehoshaphat did right except for two important omissions. One is in verse 43, and the other follows in verse 44. List them.

1.

2.

Why was making peace with Israel listed as a mark against Jehoshaphat?

Now with this introduction in mind, let's go to the first passage in 2 Chronicles 17:3-13.

Text 1/3

2 Chronicles 17:3-13 (NAS)

3 The LORD was with Jehoshaphat because he followed the example of his father David's earlier days and did not seek the Baals,

4 but sought the God of his father, followed His commandments, and did not act as Israel did.

5 So the LORD established the kingdom in his control, and all Judah brought tribute to Jehoshaphat, and he had great riches and honor.

6 He took great pride in the ways of the LORD and again removed the high places and the Asherim from Judah.

7 Then in the third year of his reign he sent his officials, ... to teach in the cities of Judah;

[. . .]

9 They taught in Judah, having the book of the law of the LORD with them; and they went throughout all the cities of Judah and taught among the people.

10 Now the dread of the LORD was on all the kingdoms of the lands which were around Judah, so that they did not make war against Jehoshaphat.

11 Some of the Philistines brought gifts and silver as tribute to Jehoshaphat; the Arabians also brought him flocks, 7,700 rams and 7,700 male goats.

12 So Jehoshaphat grew greater and greater, and he built fortresses and store cities in Judah.

13 He had large supplies in the cities of Judah, and warriors, valiant men, in Jerusalem.

Study the Text

FOCUS

FOCUS on the passage above. What FACTS are presented?

Are there any instructions to OBEY?

Do you see anything in the passage that reminds you of CHRIST?

Was there anything that was difficult to UNDERSTAND?

Are there any SINS to avoid?

Insights

In verse 3, there is a statement about Jehoshaphat that echoes what we learned about Asa. Write that statement below.

In verses 3-4, one of the keywords in Chronicles appears twice. What is that keyword?

Jehoshaphat sought and followed _____
Jehoshaphat did NOT seek or follow _____

Often when the Chronicler or the historian in Kings refers to Israel or the kings of Israel, they mean idolatry.

5 So the LORD established the kingdom in his control—Compare to Solomon in 2 Chronicles 9:13-27

5 He took great pride—Usually, we think of pride as a bad thing, but here Jehoshaphat took great pride in the ways of the Lord. The Hebrew expression is, "his heart was lifted up." Some translations render it as he "delighted" in the ways of God.

- ♦ Do you take delight in the Lord and His ways? What are some indicators that you do (or don't)? How important is it to delight in the Lord?

9 he sent his officials . . . to teach in the cities of Judah—The people of Judah were biblically illiterate, and Jehoshaphat was determined to fix that. I think he wanted his people to know God the way he did so that they, too, would delight in the Lord.

- ♦ Is biblical literacy still important? Read Matthew 28:19-20. What did Jesus expect the disciples to teach?

10 Now the dread of the LORD—Your translation may read the "fear of the Lord." The point is, because of Jehoshaphat's commitment to God, because of his emphasis that his people know and follow God, the surrounding nations decided Judah was not to be messed with.

- ♦ Does devotion to God make you more or less of a target to those who would oppose you? Does that affect your decision to be wholeheartedly committed to God?

Live the Message

Jehoshaphat placed great value on knowing God's Law. You agree that it's important, or else you wouldn't be spending time studying a long-dead Old Testament king. Not everyone agrees.

Name three reasons people are biblically illiterate.

1.

2.

3.

Are these reasons or excuses? Why would people, even people in the church, choose to remain uninformed about God and His word?

Read Psalm 119:9-16. What benefits does the psalmist list for the word of God? (If you have lots of time, Psalm 119 is one giant acrostic about the perfection of the Word of God. Each eight-verse section begins with a different Hebrew letter. Each of the 176 verses says something good about God's word.)

Do you, as a leader, affirm the importance of God's word? Do the leaders of your church hold Scripture in high regard? Does your church reflect that commitment (or lack thereof)?

Text 2/3

2 Chronicles 18:1-3, 18:28-31, 19:1-3 (NASB)

2 Chronicles 18:1-3 (NASB)

1 Now Jehoshaphat had great riches and honor; and he allied himself by marriage with Ahab.

2 Some years later he went down to visit Ahab at Samaria. And Ahab slaughtered many sheep and oxen for him and the people who were with him, and induced him to go up against Ramoth-gilead.

3 Ahab king of Israel said to Jehoshaphat king of Judah, "Will you go with me against Ramoth-gilead?" And he said to him, "I am as you are, and my people as your people, and we will be with you in the battle."

2 Chronicles 18:28-31 (NASB)

28 So the king of Israel and Jehoshaphat king of Judah went up

against Ramoth-gilead.

29 The king of Israel said to Jehoshaphat, "I will disguise myself and go into battle, but you put on your robes." So the king of Israel disguised himself, and they went into battle.

30 Now the king of Aram had commanded the captains of his chariots, saying, "Do not fight with small or great, but with the king of Israel alone."

31 So when the captains of the chariots saw Jehoshaphat, they said, "It is the king of Israel," and they turned aside to fight against him. But Jehoshaphat cried out, and the LORD helped him, and God diverted them from him.

2 Chronicles 19:1-3 (NASB)

1 Then Jehoshaphat the king of Judah returned in safety to his house in Jerusalem.

2 Jehu the son of Hanani the seer went out to meet him and said to King Jehoshaphat, "Should you help the wicked and love those who hate the LORD and so bring wrath on yourself from the LORD?

3 "But there is some good in you, for you have removed the Asheroth from the land and you have set your heart to seek God."

Study the Text

FOCUS

FOCUS on the passage above. What FACTS are presented?

Are there any instructions to OBEY?

Do you see anything in the passage that reminds you of CHRIST?

Was there anything that was difficult to UNDERSTAND?

Are there any SINS to avoid?

Insights

18:1 he allied himself by marriage with Ahab—Jehoshaphat had married his son to Ahab's daughter. This may not sound like a big deal, but remember, Ahab's name will become synonymous with wickedness and idolatry. Jehoshaphat's motives may have been pure. Perhaps he was seeking to reunify the nations. Perhaps he could argue that the young couple was genuinely in love. No matter what the justification, this will lead to disaster in Judah and Israel.

- ♦ Culturally, we expect parents to stay out of their children's romantic relationships. Is this a good thing? How involved should parents be in the choice of spouses?

18:2 And Ahab slaughtered many sheep and oxen for him and the people who were with him—Simply put, Ahab pulled out all the stops to flatter Jehoshaphat. We will find out that Jehoshaphat fell for it.

- ♦ Read Proverbs 26:28. Ahab had both a lying tongue and a flattering mouth. Why does flattery work? What kind of flattery are you most susceptible to? How can we defend against it?

18:2 induced him to go up against Ramoth-gilead—Ahab wanted to go to war with Aram (Syria) and he wanted to pull Jehoshaphat and Judah into the conflict in order to cut his own losses. Jehoshaphat was naïve and agreed to take part in a war that he had no business being in.

- How easy is it to get pulled into someone else's conflict? How do you draw the line between being supportive and meddling? Do your friends and family have a right to expect you to jump into their fights? Are there personal boundaries you should protect?

- Read Proverbs 26:17. What do you think it means by yanking a dog's ears? Does it apply to Jehoshaphat's situation?

If you read 2 Chronicles 18:4-27, you will find a further indictment of Jehoshaphat's decision to join Ahab in the upcoming battle. Jehoshaphat requests that they consult the Lord before the battle. Micaiah, the only true prophet of God, unequivocally foretells a devastating defeat for Israel. Even a clear and definitive word from God does not dissuade Jehoshaphat.

18:28 So the king of Israel and Jehoshaphat king of Judah went up against Ramoth-gilead—In spite of the clear warning from the prophet, the two kings go to battle.

- Do we ever ask God for direction, not get the answer we want, and so ignore God's instructions? Are we obligated to obey the revealed word of God?

18:29 "I will disguise myself and go into battle, but you put on your robes."—If there were any lingering questions about Ahab's character and intentions, this plan should dispel them. He intends to have Jehoshaphat draw all of the enemy's fire. And Jehoshaphat goes along with it!

- Read 2 Corinthians 6:14. Why is it dangerous to be in a partnership with an unbeliever? How do we balance engaging unbelievers with compromising our standards or disobeying God?

18:31 But Jehoshaphat cried out, and the LORD helped him, and God diverted them from him—In verse 30, the king of Aram instructs his soldiers to ignore everyone but the king of Israel, that is everyone but Ahab. (The king of Aram had obviously had dealings with Ahab before.) Because Jehoshaphat looked like a king, the Syrian soldiers attacked, placing Jehoshaphat in mortal danger. But God was gracious and rescued him.

♦ Is God obligated to bail us out? If not, why does He? Does Psalm 50:15 give any insight?

19:2 "Should you help the wicked and love those who hate the LORD and so bring wrath on yourself from the LORD?—Reminiscent of Asa being called out by Hanani the prophet, the prophet's son Jehu meets Jehoshaphat upon his return from Ramoth-gilead.

19:3 "you have set your heart to seek God"—In grace, God remembers and considers the things Jehoshaphat had done throughout his reign. Don't mistake the prophet's point. The king was not given a pass because his good deeds outweighed this one failure. Jehu was reminding the king who he was, to go back to God-honoring habits. One shortfall is not fatal. Don't let this be a habit.

♦ How do Jehu's words apply in our society where social justice is an ever-growing concern? Should the people of God be concerned with issues of justice? Is there a right way or a wrong way to pursue it?

Live the Message

Read Matthew 5:9 and Matthew 10:34. Both are the words of Jesus. How do you reconcile the two messages?

Read Romans 5:1 and continue reading Matthew 10:35-38. Do these verses shed more light?

The gospel brings peace with God because we who were His enemies are reconciled to Him. However, belonging to the kingdom of God immediately sets us in opposition against those who are outside it.

♦ Should believers pursue peace at any cost?

Text 3/3

2 Chronicles 20:2-3, 5-12, 14-18, 22-23, 27-30 (NASB)

2 Then some came and reported to Jehoshaphat, saying, "A great multitude is coming against you from beyond the sea, out of Aram and behold, they are in Hazazon-tamar (that is Engedi)."

3 Jehoshaphat was afraid and turned his attention to seek the LORD, and proclaimed a fast throughout all Judah.

[. . .]

5 Then Jehoshaphat stood in the assembly of Judah and Jerusalem, in the house of the LORD before the new court,

6 and he said, "O LORD, the God of our fathers, are You not God in the heavens? And are You not ruler over all the kingdoms of the nations? Power and might are in Your hand so that no one can stand against You.

7 "Did You not, O our God, drive out the inhabitants of this land before Your people Israel and give it to the descendants of Abraham Your friend forever?

8 "They have lived in it, and have built You a sanctuary there for Your name, saying,

9 'Should evil come upon us, the sword, or judgment, or pestilence, or famine, we will stand before this house and before You (for Your name is in this house) and cry to You in our distress, and You will

hear and deliver us.'

10 "Now behold, the sons of Ammon and Moab and Mount Seir, whom You did not let Israel invade when they came out of the land of Egypt (they turned aside from them and did not destroy them),

11 see how they are rewarding us by coming to drive us out from Your possession which You have given us as an inheritance.

12 "O our God, will You not judge them? For we are powerless before this great multitude who are coming against us; nor do we know what to do, but our eyes are on You."

[...]

14 Then in the midst of the assembly the Spirit of the LORD came upon Jahaziel the son of Zechariah, the son of Benaiah, the son of Jeiel, the son of Mattaniah, the Levite of the sons of Asaph;

15 and he said, "Listen, all Judah and the inhabitants of Jerusalem and King Jehoshaphat: thus says the LORD to you, 'Do not fear or be dismayed because of this great multitude, for the battle is not yours but God's.

16 'Tomorrow go down against them. Behold, they will come up by the ascent of Ziz, and you will find them at the end of the valley in front of the wilderness of Jeruel.

17 'You need not fight in this battle; station yourselves, stand and see the salvation of the LORD on your behalf, O Judah and Jerusalem.' Do not fear or be dismayed; tomorrow go out to face them, for the LORD is with you."

18 Jehoshaphat bowed his head with his face to the ground, and all Judah and the inhabitants of Jerusalem fell down before the LORD, worshiping the LORD.

[...]

22 When they began singing and praising, the LORD set ambushes against the sons of Ammon, Moab and Mount Seir, who had come against Judah; so they were routed.

23 For the sons of Ammon and Moab rose up against the inhabitants of Mount Seir destroying them completely; and when they had finished with the inhabitants of Seir, they helped to destroy one another.

[...]

27 Every man of Judah and Jerusalem returned with Jehoshaphat at their head, returning to Jerusalem with joy, for the LORD had made them to rejoice over their enemies.

28 They came to Jerusalem with harps, lyres and trumpets to the house of the LORD.

29 And the dread of God was on all the kingdoms of the lands when they heard that the LORD had fought against the enemies of Israel.

30 So the kingdom of Jehoshaphat was at peace, for his God gave him rest on all sides.

Study the Text

FOCUS

FOCUS on the passage above. What FACTS are presented?

Are there any instructions to OBEY?

Do you see anything in the passage that reminds you of CHRIST?

Was there anything that was difficult to UNDERSTAND?

Are there any SINS to avoid?

Insights

2 **"A great multitude is coming against you"**—This army may have been emboldened by the debacle at Ramoth-gilead. If so, that is a somber reminder that our actions don't happen in a vacuum. The world is watching.

3 Jehoshaphat was afraid and turned his attention to seek the LORD, and proclaimed a fast—Fear is not necessarily a sign of cowardice. Sometimes it is a perfectly reasonable response to a legitimate threat. But Jehoshaphat didn't let his fear paralyze him. On the contrary, it prompted action. What two actions did Jehoshaphat take?

1.

2.

6-7 Jehoshaphat takes the lead in prayer. In these verses, he bases his appeal to God on four things.

1.

2.

3.

4.

♦ How important is it to rehearse these four things when we seek God's intervention?

10-11—Jehoshaphat recounts that when Israel left Egypt, God would not allow them to invade or otherwise harm the enemies now mustering against them. This is patently unfair, and it makes the nations' belligerence now all the more disheartening.

♦ How do you usually react when your fairness is rewarded with a stab in the back? Read Hebrews 12:3 and Hebrews 4:15. Does knowing Jesus "gets it" change how we endure mistreatment?

12 "O our God, will You not judge them? For we are powerless before this great multitude who are coming against us; nor do we know what to do, but our eyes are on You."—Jehoshaphat appeals to God's own sense of justice and then surrenders the situation.

♦ Letting go of tough situations is often very hard for us to do.

Why do you think that is?

17 "station yourselves, stand and see the salvation of the LORD on your behalf,"—God responds very quickly through the Levite, Jahaziel. He gives three simple instructions

1.

2.

3.

Compare this to Exodus 14:13-14.

18 Jehoshaphat . . . and all Judah . . . fell down before the LORD, worshiping the LORD.—On the promise of victory, Jehoshaphat and the nation worships God.

- ♦ It is a statement of faith to celebrate the victory before it actually happens. When do we celebrate God's victories? Do we celebrate them? Could it be that we don't see God's intervention as often because we do not approach it in faith and don't honor God afterward?

22 When they began singing and praising, the LORD set ambushes—In the middle of Judah's worship, God is working on their behalf.

27 Every man of Judah . . . returned . . . with joy, for the LORD had made them to rejoice over their enemies—Judah had depended on God in faith. They had worshiped Him and now they return in joy and victory.

29 And the dread of God was on all the kingdoms of the lands when

they heard that the LORD had fought against the enemies of Israel.

♦ Do we still see great victories like this one? Does the LORD still fight against our enemies? Read James 4:1-2. How much time and energy do we expend fighting each other?

Live the Message

Judah never gave in to their fears because of Jehoshaphat's faith. He provided exactly the kind of leadership and example they needed. But think for a moment and write down a definition for faith.

Read Hebrews 11:1, which gives one definition.

What does James 1:6 say about faith?

Now consider 1 John 5:4 and Revelation 12:10—12a. What kind of faith do the believers exhibit? What results when we exercise that kind of faith?

How is faith in God different from blind faith?

Jehoshaphat's Legacy

When a man's ways are pleasing to the LORD, He makes even his enemies to be at peace with him. Proverbs 16:7 (NASB)

This seems to sum up Jehoshaphat. His ways, his daily life, and his routines were pleasing to the LORD because he worked against idolatry and put an emphasis on the word of God. He knew his people couldn't or wouldn't obey a law they didn't know.

Jehoshaphat was human and not perfect. We saw his blind spot—cooperation with Judah's enemies, and by extension, the enemies of God. He teaches us we need to be aware that we have blind spots and be vigilant not to let them harm our walk.

The king learned his lesson, though, and humbly, boldly led his nation to faith-filled reliance on God even in the most desperate situation.

Review the passage and your notes. What did you learn? How do those lessons speak to your life? Record them here. Also check pages 103-105.

Next Session

Unfortunately, Jehoshaphat's son, Jehoram, seemed to draw more from his father-in-law, Ahab, and the kings of Israel than he did from his godly father. Once Jehoram was firmly established as king, he had all his brothers executed.

That foments a period of bloody unrest and uncertainty that lasts until Jehoram's seven-year-old grandson, Joash, is crowned. In the next session, we'll look at what we can learn from a child king.

Joash–The Insincere King

Prepare

Gather your study materials—Bible, notebook, pens, and pencils. Settle into your favorite study spot. Take a few moments to ready your heart and mind and detach from the concerns of your daily routine. You are preparing to enter the presence of God, and He has something to say to you. Make sure you are ready to hear it.

Open your study time with prayer. Ask the Holy Spirit to help renew your passion for serving God. "Lord, You deserve my undivided attention and commitment. Keep me from laziness and from following You out of habit or routine."

♦ What motivates you to live a godly life?

Text 1/3

2 Chronicles 22:10-12 (NIV)

10 When Athaliah the mother of Ahaziah saw that her son was dead, she proceeded to destroy the whole royal family of the house of Judah.

11 But Jehosheba, the daughter of King Jehoram, took Joash son of Ahaziah and stole him away from among the royal princes who were about to be murdered and put him and his nurse in a bedroom. Because Jehosheba, the daughter of King Jehoram and wife of the priest Jehoiada, was Ahaziah's sister, she hid the child from Athaliah so she could not kill him.

12 He remained hidden with them at the temple of God for six years while Athaliah ruled the land.

2 Chronicles 24:1-5a (NIV)

1 Joash was seven years old when he became king, and he reigned in Jerusalem forty years. His mother's name was Zibiah; she was

from Beersheba.

2 Joash did what was right in the eyes of the LORD all the years of Jehoiada the priest.

3 Jehoiada chose two wives for him, and he had sons and daughters.

4 Some time later Joash decided to restore the temple of the LORD.

5 He called together the priests and Levites and said to them, "Go to the towns of Judah and collect the money due annually from all Israel, to repair the temple of your God. Do it now."

Study the Text

FOCUS

FOCUS on the passage above. What FACTS are presented?

Are there any instructions to OBEY?

Do you see anything in the passage that reminds you of CHRIST?

Was there anything that was difficult to UNDERSTAND?

Are there any SINS to avoid?

Insights

10 she proceeded to destroy the whole royal family of the house of

Judah—Her first act was to destroy—that is, execute—everyone else with a claim to the throne. This included her grandchildren, along with any of her son's half-brothers or uncles. Imagine that.

- ◆ Read 2 Samuel 7:16. What promise does God make to David?

11 But Jehosheba, the daughter of King Jehoram, took Joash son of Ahaziah and . . . hid the child from Athaliah so she could not kill him.—Jehosheba, half-sister of Athalia's dead son, hid her infant nephew. This act took discernment and bold courage.

- ◆ Sometimes one person's courage makes the difference in the kingdom of God. Are you facing a situation right now that requires courage? Are you acting with courage?

12 while Athaliah ruled the land.—The Chronicler doesn't give any details of Athaliah's reign, which is his way of indicating that she was an illegitimate ruler. What made her rule illegitimate?

In 2 Chronicles 23 and 2 Kings 11, you can read details of how Jehosheba's husband, the priest Jehoiada, assembled a loyal group who overthrew Athaliah and installed seven-year-old Joash as king.

2 Chronicles 23:16 sets the tone.

- ◆ Jehoiada then made a covenant that he and the people and the king would be the LORD's people.

- ◆ Do you think it was difficult for Jehosheba, Jehoiada, and the others to wait for more than six long years for this plan to work itself out?

- ◆ Read 1 Corinthians 1:27. Does this give any insight into

Joash's coronation?

24:2 Joash did what was right in the eyes of the LORD all the years of Jehoiada the priest.—The writer is careful to say "all the years of Jehoiada."

♦ How is this assessment different from the comments on Jehoshaphat and Asa?

3 Jehoiada chose two wives for him—It is absolutely true that having multiple wives is outside God's plan. Without weaseling too much, the text does not necessarily say that Joash was married to both at the same time. He may have been widowed. However, the takeaway is how much Joash trusted Jehoiada's advice. He deferred to his mentor on the most important decision in his life.

♦ We need mentors and we need to be mentors. This is the way Christ worked with His disciples and it is the way Paul trained young ministers. Why do you think this system works well? Are you being mentored? Who are you mentoring?

4 Some time later Joash decided to restore the temple of the LORD.— Joash was not Jehoiada's puppet. This was his own decision. The undertaking lasted into the second half of his reign. This shows it wasn't a passing whim. If you look at the verses following our FOCUS passage, you'll see that Joash stayed on his staff, the priests, and Levites to get the job done.

It is easy to come up with great projects, works that need to be done. It is another thing to muster and maintain the energy and drive to accomplish them. Read 2 Corinthians 8:11. How do Paul's words relate?

♦ What kind of witness is it if we don't finish what we start?

Live the Message

Consider the two women in the passages. What motivated each of them to act? What motivates you to move from talking and thinking to bold action? Is there a bold action you need to take now?

Joash spent his early reign on the Temple renovation. Do you have an intense desire to restore, to revive your worship? Do you long to meet with God, to be where He meets with His people? Are you generous with our contributions so that His full glory can be made known?

Text 2/3

2 Chronicles 24:15-22 (NIV)

15 Now Jehoiada was old and full of years, and he died at the age of a hundred and thirty.

16 He was buried with the kings in the City of David, because of the good he had done in Israel for God and his temple.

17 After the death of Jehoiada, the officials of Judah came and paid homage to the king, and he listened to them.

18 They abandoned the temple of the LORD, the God of their fathers, and worshiped Asherah poles and idols. Because of their guilt, God's anger came upon Judah and Jerusalem.

19 Although the LORD sent prophets to the people to bring them back to him, and though they testified against them, they would not listen.

20 Then the Spirit of God came upon Zechariah son of Jehoiada the priest. He stood before the people and said, "This is what God says: 'Why do you disobey the LORD's commands? You will not prosper.

Because you have forsaken the LORD, he has forsaken you.'"

21 But they plotted against him, and by order of the king they stoned him to death in the courtyard of the LORD's temple.

22 King Joash did not remember the kindness Zechariah's father Jehoiada had shown him but killed his son, who said as he lay dying, "May the LORD see this and call you to account."

Study the Text

FOCUS

FOCUS on the passage above. What FACTS are presented?

Are there any instructions to OBEY?

Do you see anything in the passage that reminds you of CHRIST?

Was there anything that was difficult to UNDERSTAND?

Are there any SINS to avoid?

Insights

15 Jehoiada died at the age of a hundred and thirty—Whoa. One hundred and thirty is old, no matter what the circumstances. We get the impression that Jehoiada was still active in service to God and the king.

54

- Do believers ever retire from God's service?

16 He was buried with the kings in the City of David—It is a testimony to Jehoiada's life and influence that he was afforded the singular honor of being buried with the kings.

- Think of the largest funerals in recent memory. Who were they for? Do large funerals indicate what we value as a society? If so, what then, do we value?

17 the officials of Judah came and paid homage to the king—We don't have a lot of details about who these guys are. The most reasonable speculation is that they may have been bureaucrats left from Athaliah's reign. With the old priest gone, they saw a window of opportunity to return to power and influence.

- What is a power vacuum? Is it possible to have one in a church? Is there any way to insulate the body from it?

17 [Joash] listened to them—Joash may have been a little uncertain, insecure now that his lifelong advisor was gone. The flattery these officials laid down worked on the young king with disastrous efficiency.

- Read Ephesians 4:11-14. How do we keep the church from being infiltrated and controlled by self-seeking, false doctrine?

18 They abandoned the temple of the LORD, the God of their fathers—The ultimate goal for the officials was the re-establishing of idolatry in Judah. And notice, it wasn't in addition to the worship of Yahweh. It was instead of. Joash turned his back on what had been his life's work.

- Read Matthew 6:24. While Jesus is specifically talking about money as the second master, does the principle hold true? Do we ever try to serve two masters? What inevitably happens?

18 Because of their guilt—Guilt. The officials and the king are held accountable for their actions.

19 LORD sent prophets to the people to bring them back to him— Notice how God responds to the clearly established guilt of the king and his officials. God reaches out to them in grace, sending prophets to draw them back to Him.

- Can you remember a time when God spoke to you in grace in spite of your rebellion? Read Psalm 103:8-14 and record your reflections.

- The prophet Joel was active during Joash's reign. Read Joel 2:12-13. Consider how this message might have applied.

20 Then the Spirit of God came upon Zechariah son of Jehoiada the priest—There is a sense that if Joash would hear anyone, it would be the son of his beloved mentor. Now, if Jehoiada recently died at the age of a hundred and thirty, Zechariah is no doubt mature himself.

Zechariah's words reflect God's warning in Deuteronomy 31:16-17. What did God predict?

21 But they plotted against him, and by order of the king they stoned him to death in the courtyard of the LORD's temple.—I'll be honest. This makes my jaw drop. By order of the king. Stoned him to death, by implication as a false prophet in the courtyard of the Temple. This is the definition of a heinous crime. In Luke 11:47-51, Jesus Himself condemns the Jews for the outrage of killing God's prophets from Abel to Zechariah, from A to Z and from Genesis to 2 Chronicles, which was the last book in the Hebrew Bible. It is a breathtaking indictment.

22 King Joash did not remember the kindness—More accurately, Joash willfully ignored the kindness. Ironically, the murder takes place in the same spot Joash was crowned king years before.

22 "May the LORD see this and call you to account."—Zechariah's dying words. While the murder needs to be avenged, these men executed God's own Spirit-anointed messenger. It is an affront, an attack on God Himself.

♦ Read Stephen's dying words in Acts 7:60. Why does Stephen ask for his killers' forgiveness while Zechariah calls for accountability? Is Stephen just a better person? Is it an Old Testament versus New Testament thing? (Hint: No.) Compare with Revelation 6:10.

The Hebrew word translated "call you to account" is the same word the Chronicler uses for when he speaks of seeking the Lord. Joash abandoned seeking the Lord, so now the Lord would seek the king, for judgment.

Live the Message

In verse 19, God sent prophets to bring the people back to Him. That's what He has been doing since the Garden of Eden. Read 2 Corinthians 5:18-20. How do we fit into God's great purpose?

Consider 1 John 2:19 in light of what you have read about Joash. What does this verse mean for the message or ministry of reconciliation we have been entrusted with?

Text 3/3

2 Kings 12:17-18 (NIV)

17 About this time Hazael king of Aram went up and attacked Gath and captured it. Then he turned to attack Jerusalem.

18 But Joash king of Judah took all the sacred objects dedicated by his fathers—Jehoshaphat, Jehoram and Ahaziah, the kings of Judah—and the gifts he himself had dedicated and all the gold found in the treasuries of the temple of the LORD and of the royal palace, and he sent them to Hazael king of Aram, who then withdrew from Jerusalem.

2 Chronicles 24:23-25 (NIV)

23 At the turn of the year, the army of Aram marched against Joash; it invaded Judah and Jerusalem and killed all the leaders of the people. They sent all the plunder to their king in Damascus.

24 Although the Aramean army had come with only a few men, the LORD delivered into their hands a much larger army. Because Judah had forsaken the LORD, the God of their fathers, judgment was executed on Joash.

25 When the Arameans withdrew, they left Joash severely wounded. His officials conspired against him for murdering the son of Jehoiada the priest, and they killed him in his bed. So he died and was buried in the City of David, but not in the tombs of the kings.

Study the Text

FOCUS

FOCUS on the passages above. What FACTS are presented?

Are there any instructions to OBEY?

Do you see anything in the passage that reminds you of CHRIST?

Was there anything that was difficult to UNDERSTAND?

Are there any SINS to avoid?

Insights

The best resolution for Kings and Chronicles is that the accounts are two separate incidents. Hazael came to Gath and had designs on Jerusalem. Joash bribed him, and he went away. The next spring, however, he returned and attacked. With that sequence in mind, let's look at these few verses.

Remember that peace in the land is a sign of the king's right relationship before God, while war with enemies reflects God's withdrawal of favor. Joash is facing the military advance of Aram.

1 Kings 12:18 all the sacred objects . . . all the gold found in the treasuries of the temple of the LORD and of the royal palace—After spending years leading the people to re-establish the Mosaic offerings and collections, Joash himself plunders them.

- ♦ Flip back to the previous passage and reread Zechariah's message. What does the word "prosper" mean?

18 and the gifts he himself had dedicated—In sin and in panic, Joash undoes the good deeds he had done previously.

- ♦ Read Psalm 34:12-19 and think about how it applies to Joash. Does the passage advocate peace at any price? How does that fit with the verse we looked at with Jehoshaphat, Proverbs 16:7? Was peace with Aram possible? Why or why not?

2 Chronicles 24: 23 At the turn of the year—Spring was when kings went to war. You may recall David got into trouble with Bathsheba because he was in Jerusalem in the spring while his army was in the field. In the spring, the weather was dry. The winter harvest was in. This little detail demonstrates that Hazael planned this attack. It wasn't a whim or a spur of the moment campaign.

23 killed all the leaders of the people—It would seems that these are the same leaders who persuaded Joash to embrace the worship of pagan gods. Again the judgment predicted by Zechariah has fallen.

- ♦ Read Luke 17:26-30. While Jesus is speaking in the context of His return, what do these verses tell you about God's judgment? Does He give warnings? Is it immediate? How does this apply to our current age?

24 the Aramean army had come with only a few men, the LORD delivered into their hands a much larger army—God is sovereign. As much as we would like to think it is our bravery or our brilliant strategies that win battles, it is the Lord.

- ♦ God never does things randomly. What purpose does defeat serve?

24 judgment was executed on Joash—Make no mistake, this is invasion was not simply the outworking of ancient geopolitics. Notice the leaders, especially Joash are held accountable.

- ♦ Why does God have the right to bring judgment in Joash (or anyone else)? Read Isaiah 43:10-13

25 they left Joash severely wounded. His officials conspired against him for murdering the son of Jehoiada the priest, and they killed him in his bed.—Joash was weak and unable to defend himself and the conspirators seized that moment.

♦ Is this assassination just or unjust? Why? Does Daniel 4:25 offer any insight?

♦ Does this mean we must simply endure unjust or oppressive rulers? Read Romans 13:1 and Acts 4:19 and 1 Peter 2:13-17. Do these principles only apply in monarchies or authoritarian governments?

25 but not in the tombs of the kings—The hope Judah had at Joash's crowning came to an ignominious end. No honor for this apostate king.

Live the Message

What is apostasy? Think about your church. How many people used to be regular attenders but are no longer there? What happened?

We could make a case that Joash was following a person (Jehoiada) rather than God Himself. How prevalent is this in the church today?

Read 2 Timothy 4:2-5. What does that tell you about human nature and our response to the gospel message?

Three more references: Mark 13:13, Hebrews 3:6, 3:14, and Galatians 5:22-23. Do genuine believers abandon their faith?

Joash's Legacy

Joash's legacy is a sad one. Such a great beginning, with God's hand so evidently working in his life, to an end of breathtaking arrogance and sin. Unfortunately his story is a familiar one. Reading his story, we would do well to remember the words attributed to the English reformer and martyr, William Bradford, "There but for the grace of God go I."

Take the study of Joash as an opportunity to settle in your mind who God is and reaffirm your commitment to serve Him.

Review the passage and your notes. What did you learn? How do those lessons speak to your life? Record them here. Also check pages 103-105.

Next Session

In the next session, Joash's son, Amaziah, begins his reign dealing with the fallout from his father's assassination. But we'll see Joash's lack of commitment to God will influence his son.

5

Amaziah—The Inscrutable King

Prepare

Gather your study materials—Bible, notebook, pens, and pencils. Settle into your favorite study spot. Pour your coffee or grab your snacks. What did Paul mean when he gave these instructions: "Do not be unequally yoked together with unbelievers. For what fellowship has righteousness with lawlessness? And what communion has light with darkness?" 2 Corinthians 6:14 (NKJV)

Open your study time with prayer. Ask the Holy Spirit to help you approach the study with wisdom and discernment. Be open to His prodding when there are areas that need work.

♦ Should we seek help from anyone willing to offer it?

The account of Amaziah in 2 Kings 14 is a more condensed version of the 2 Chronicles 25 version. As a result, we are only going to examine 2 Chronicles.

Text 1/3

2 Chronicles 25:1-4 (NKJV)

1 Amaziah was twenty-five years old when he became king, and he reigned twenty-nine years in Jerusalem. His mother's name was Jehoaddan of Jerusalem.

2 And he did what was right in the sight of the LORD, but not with a loyal heart.

3 Now it happened, as soon as the kingdom was established for him, that he executed his servants who had murdered his father the

king.

4 However he did not execute their children, but did as it is written in the Law in the Book of Moses, where the LORD commanded, saying, "The fathers shall not be put to death for their children, nor shall the children be put to death for their fathers; but a person shall die for his own sin."

Study the Text

FOCUS

FOCUS on the passage above. What FACTS are presented?

Are there any instructions to OBEY?

Do you see anything in the passage that reminds you of CHRIST?

Was there anything that was difficult to UNDERSTAND?

Are there any SINS to avoid?

Insights

2 but not with a loyal heart—This is also rendered not wholeheartedly. This is lip service. It is a sign that Amaziah found something else more compelling.

- ♦ In 1 Kings 11:4, we find Solomon was the first king with divided loyalties, resulting in a divided kingdom. Why do you suppose the later kings did not learn from Solomon's example?

3 he executed his servants who had murdered his father the king—
Now the first part of the verse says "when Amaziah was established as king," he carried out the ordained penalty under the Mosaic Law for murder. It was not a rash act. It was not pure vengeance. This is important because it shows Amaziah was capable of thoughtful action. Remember this later in his reign.

- Read Proverbs 25:5. Why was this sentencing important for the young king? Are there other situations when dealing decisively with sins is important?

4 but did as it is written in the Law in the Book of Moses—It is beyond our understanding of justice that anyone would consider sentencing children to death for the crimes of the parents. However, it was very common at that time, especially in pagan societies. For example, in Esther 7:10 and 9:13, Haman and his ten sons were hanged for his crimes.

- Read Ezekiel 18:20-32. It's a little long, but what does it tell you about God's take on judgment?

Live the Message

In holding only his father's assassins guilty, Amaziah went against culture and expectations to uphold God's Law and His standards. Read 1 Peter 4:4-5. What is our relationship to culture? What methods does the culture use to enforce conformity?

Read 1 Timothy 6:11-16. What is the motivation for not living like the rest of the world? Is that adequate motivation for you? Why or why not?

Text 2/3

2 Chronicles 25:5-12 (NKJV)

5 Moreover Amaziah gathered Judah together and set over them captains of thousands and captains of hundreds, according to their fathers' houses, throughout all Judah and Benjamin; and he numbered them from twenty years old and above, and found them to be three hundred thousand choice men, able to go to war, who could handle spear and shield.

6 He also hired one hundred thousand mighty men of valor from Israel for one hundred talents of silver.

7 But a man of God came to him, saying, "O king, do not let the army of Israel go with you, for the LORD is not with Israel—not with any of the children of Ephraim.

8 But if you go, be gone! Be strong in battle! Even so, God shall make you fall before the enemy; for God has power to help and to overthrow."

9 Then Amaziah said to the man of God, "But what shall we do about the hundred talents which I have given to the troops of Israel?" And the man of God answered, "The LORD is able to give you much more than this."

10 So Amaziah discharged the troops that had come to him from Ephraim, to go back home. Therefore their anger was greatly aroused against Judah, and they returned home in great anger.

11 Then Amaziah strengthened himself, and leading his people, he went to the Valley of Salt and killed ten thousand of the people of Seir.

12 Also the children of Judah took captive ten thousand alive, brought them to the top of the rock, and cast them down from the top of the rock, so that they all were dashed in pieces.

Study the Text

FOCUS

FOCUS on the passage above. What FACTS are presented?

Are there any instructions to OBEY?

Do you see anything in the passage that reminds you of CHRIST?

Was there anything that was difficult to UNDERSTAND?

Are there any SINS to avoid?

Insights

5 three hundred thousand choice men—We need some background here. The nation of Edom had been pushing back against Judah since the reign of Jehoshaphat. In a few verses, we'll see that Edom is the target of this military mobilization. The important thing is the size of the army. In 2 Chronicles 17:14-19, Jehoshaphat's army numbered over a million troops. Amaziah can only muster less than a third of that.

♦ Judah had not suffered a significant decrease in population. Why do you suppose the size of the army dropped off so much? How much does the size of the army actually matter?

6 He also hired one hundred thousand mighty men of valor from

Israel for one hundred talents of silver.—Amaziah evidently felt the pressure and enlisted mercenaries. If the talent is the commonly accepted seventy-five pounds, then Amaziah paid over $2.5 million (US) to these guys.

- ♦ We can only speculate on Amaziah's motives for spending so much to hire these extra soldiers. That said, why do people put themselves in financial jeopardy?

7 do not let the army of Israel go with you, for the LORD is not with Israel—And unnamed prophet issues a stern warning to the king about his mercenaries.

- ♦ Read Numbers 14:42-43. Why did God abandon the northern kingdom of Israel?

8 Even so, God shall make you fall before the enemy;—The original Hebrew for the first part of verse 8 is difficult to translate, so they range from "Even if you go and fight bravely, you will fall," to an almost sarcastic rendering: "Sure. Suit yourself. Go and fight, but it's going to end badly."

8 for God has power to help and to overthrow.—In our study up to now, we have seen both.

- ♦ Read Psalm 20:7 and Isaiah 31:1. Then compare Jeremiah 17:5-8. Does it matter who you look to for help?

9 But what shall we do about the hundred talents which I have given to the troops of Israel?—Amaziah reveals his character and his heart. Yes, he is talking about a huge sum of money, but he is a man willing to obey God, but he wants to cut his losses.

- ♦ Amaziah's hesitation is actually very relatable. Read Deuteronomy 8:17-18. Is it easier to trust God to win a battle than to provide financially? How does this financial insecurity impact the body of Christ?

10 they returned home in great anger—The man of God convinces Amaziah, and he dismisses the mercenaries. They pocket around $250, but they lose the opportunity to plunder Edom. They promptly reveal their character and motivation. In verse 13, the plunder some of the cities in Judah on the way home and kill 3,000 innocent people.

- ♦ How do you respond when things don't work out the way you want or expect?

11 Then Amaziah strengthened himself, and leading his people, he went to the Valley of Salt—The king led his army to victory, but in verse 12, his cruelty is exposed.

- ♦ Success sometimes reveals more about our true selves than failure. What do Amaziah's actions reveal about him? Read James 3:13. What can you say about Amaziah? How do you measure up to James's standard?

Live the Message

One of the things Amaziah did correctly was to listen (albeit begrudgingly) to the prophet's godly counsel. The counsel was counterintuitive for sure. More soldiers have to be better, right? Except that it wasn't. How do you decide who to listen to?

Go back to James 3:13 and read through verses 13-18. Contrast "good" wisdom versus "worldly" wisdom. Where does worldly wisdom ultimately originate?

What will you use as a test to determine what kind of wisdom or counsel you're receiving?

Our culture is very socially active and justice-oriented. When Jesus proclaimed the beginning of His ministry in Luke 4:18-19, He mentioned His mission would include things that are familiar to us— ministering to the poor and oppressed.

In our society, there is no end to needs and opportunities to serve. Prison reform. Addiction intervention. Ending exploitation. Caring for immigrants. And many, many others.

The question for us, is should we—as believers—partner with anyone else to accomplish these objectives? Can the church separate the social needs and opportunities from the gospel?

We previously looked at 2 Corinthians 6:14 and being unequally yoked with unbelievers. Now read Ezra 4:1-3. Can you, should you trust everyone who offers to help in your cause?

The disciples encountered a similar situation in Mark 9:38-40. Many years after this, John wrote in his first letter. A complete study of 1 John is a task for another day. But look at 1 John 1:6-7 and 1 John 2:15-16. What are some things to look for and avoid when choosing who to cooperate with?

Text 3/3

2 Chronicles 25:14-27 (NKJV)

14 Now it was so, after Amaziah came from the slaughter of the Edomites, that he brought the gods of the people of Seir, set them up to be his gods, and bowed down before them and burned incense to them.

15 Therefore the anger of the LORD was aroused against Amaziah, and He sent him a prophet who said to him, "Why have you sought the gods of the people, which could not rescue their own people from your hand?"

16 So it was, as he talked with him, that the king said to him, "Have we made you the king's counselor? Cease! Why should you be killed?" Then the prophet ceased, and said, "I know that God has determined to destroy you, because you have done this and have not heeded my advice."

17 Now Amaziah king of Judah asked advice and sent to Joash the son of Jehoahaz, the son of Jehu, king of Israel, saying, "Come, let us face one another in battle."

18 And Joash king of Israel sent to Amaziah king of Judah, saying, "The thistle that was in Lebanon sent to the cedar that was in Lebanon, saying, 'Give your daughter to my son as wife'; and a wild beast that was in Lebanon passed by and trampled the thistle.

19 Indeed you say that you have defeated the Edomites, and your heart is lifted up to boast. Stay at home now; why should you meddle with trouble, that you should fall—you and Judah with you?"

20 But Amaziah would not heed, for it came from God, that He might give them into the hand of their enemies, because they sought the gods of Edom.

21 So Joash king of Israel went out; and he and Amaziah king of Judah faced one another at Beth Shemesh, which belongs to Judah.

22 And Judah was defeated by Israel, and every man fled to his tent.

23 Then Joash the king of Israel captured Amaziah king of Judah, the son of Joash, the son of Jehoahaz, at Beth Shemesh; and he brought him to Jerusalem, and broke down the wall of Jerusalem from the Gate of Ephraim to the Corner Gate—four hundred cubits.

24 And he took all the gold and silver, all the articles that were found in the house of God with Obed-Edom, the treasures of the

king's house, and hostages, and returned to Samaria.

[...]

27 After the time that Amaziah turned away from following the LORD, they made a conspiracy against him in Jerusalem, and he fled to Lachish; but they sent after him to Lachish and killed him there.

Study the Text

FOCUS

FOCUS on the passage above. What FACTS are presented?

Are there any instructions to OBEY?

Do you see anything in the passage that reminds you of CHRIST?

Was there anything that was difficult to UNDERSTAND?

Are there any SINS to avoid?

Insights

14 that he brought the gods of the people of Seir, set them up to be his gods, and bowed down before them and burned incense to them—Taking a defeated people's idols away was a common practice. It communicated the gods' powerlessness and the people's vulnerability as long as they worshiped their idols. When Amaziah adopts those idols as his gods and worships them . . . There is no rational explanation.

♦ Some have reasoned that Amaziah's victory made him especially susceptible to Satan's attacks. Look at 1 Corinthians 10:12. What does it tell you about temptation?

15 Why have you sought the gods of the people—Ironically, this is the same word, sought, that we've seen throughout Chronicles but in the context of seeking God.

♦ Have you ever turned to something else for comfort, for reassurance, for confidence apart from God? It may not be a statue, but it is idolatry, nonetheless. Do you suppose that is why God's commandment against idolatry is the first one He gave?

16 "Have we made you the king's counselor? Cease! Why should you be killed?"—Amaziah essentially replies, "I don't recall asking for your advice." Then the king threatens him with death. He no doubt remembered his father's execution of Zechariah, the prophet.

♦ Want to identify your idols? What will you take extreme measures to protect? What will cause you to fight when it's threatened? (Now, I'm not talking about fighting off a physical attacker who's threatening you or your family. But rather, what makes you defensive?)

16 I know that God has determined to destroy you, because you have done this and have not heeded my advice.—The prophet's words are chilling. List the two reasons God has determined to destroy the king.

1.

2.

- It is breathtakingly arrogant to sin against God, but then to ignore His clear warnings and correction is stunning. Read Hebrews 10:28-29. Why are people so bold in their sin?

17 Now Amaziah king of Judah asked advice and sent to Joash the son of Jehoahaz, the son of Jehu, king of Israel, saying, "Come, let us face one another in battle."—Fresh off his victory over Edom, with his new gods, and advisors who were not men of God, Amaziah picks a fight with Joash (he's also called Jehoash, not the guy we just studied), the king of Israel.

- Are we more likely to surround ourselves with people who challenge us or who echo our own thoughts? Read Proverbs 27:6. Does it apply here?

19 "Indeed you say that you have defeated the Edomites, and your heart is lifted up to boast. Stay at home now; why should you meddle with trouble, that you should fall—you and Judah with you?"—Underline the key phrase in Jehoash's reply.

20 for it came from God . . . because they sought the gods of Edom—God will follow through.

- Read Romans 9:22-23. Why does God's anger make us uncomfortable? How does it relate to His love and mercy?

23 Then Joash the king of Israel captured Amaziah king of Judah—Read verses 22-24 and list three major results of the battle of Beth Shemesh.

1.

2.

3.

This is a preview/object lesson for Judah. Within two hundred years, Babylon will begin taking the people of Judah captive and will eventually destroy Jerusalem, all as judgment for Judah's idolatry.

♦ Does history repeat itself? Why or why not?

27 After the time that Amaziah turned away from following the LORD, they made a conspiracy against him in Jerusalem, and he fled to Lachish; but they sent after him to Lachish and killed him there.— A sad ending to Amaziah's life and reign.

While murder is not justified, what might be the motive for the assassination?

Live the Message

Do we want godly counsel? Do you want godly counsel?

How often do we expect godly counsel to conform to what we already think? (That is, how often do we want "godly counsel" to validate what we've already decided?)

Consider Proverbs 12:26 and Proverbs 27:17. How should you choose your close friends or those whose advice you'll listen to?

Why are times of victory or personal success so dangerous for us in our walk with Christ?

Read Joshua 1:8 and John 15:5. Where does success come from?

In 2 Timothy 4:7-8, how does Paul define success?

Do we, does the church, need a change in perspective on success?

Besides Amaziah, who paid the price for his arrogance?

Amaziah's Legacy

Amaziah makes me shake my head. Why on earth would he follow the same path his father did? It seems like he didn't learn anything. Perhaps that's what makes him so relatable. Unfortunately. He shows us we can't be lazy in our commitment to God. We can't phone it in. The consequences are devastating.

Review the passage and your notes. What did you learn? How do those lessons speak to your life? Record them here. Also check pages 103-105.

Next Session

Amaziah's son, Uzziah (Azariah), becomes king as a sixteen-year-old and enjoys the longest reign in Judah's history. Will he break the cycle of lazy commitment and late apostasy?

6

Uzziah—The Presumptuous King

Prepare

Before diving into this session, take a moment and think of the kings we've studied. What have you learned? What has God brought to your attention? As you gather your materials and settle into your favorite study spot, thank God for personally instructing you. Commit to listening with an open heart and mind going forward.

Which is more dangerous spiritually—failure or success? Why?

Uzziah is only mentioned in passing in 2 Kings. Therefore, as with his father, Amaziah, we will focus on the 2 Chronicles record. Although the readings are short, we can learn some important truths.

Text 1/3

2 Chronicles 26:1-5 (CSB)

> 1 All the people of Judah took Uzziah, who was sixteen years old, and made him king in place of his father Amaziah.
>
> 2 After Amaziah the king rested with his ancestors, Uzziah rebuilt Eloth and restored it to Judah.
>
> 3 Uzziah was sixteen years old when he became king, and he reigned fifty-two years in Jerusalem. His mother's name was Jecoliah; she was from Jerusalem.
>
> 4 He did what was right in the LORD's sight just as his father Amaziah had done.
>
> 5 He sought God throughout the lifetime of Zechariah, the teacher of the fear of God. During the time that he sought the Lord, God gave

him success.

Study the Text

FOCUS

FOCUS on the passage above. What FACTS are presented?

Are there any instructions to OBEY?

Do you see anything in the passage that reminds you of CHRIST?

Was there anything that was difficult to UNDERSTAND?

Are there any SINS to avoid?

Insights

1 All the people of Judah took Uzziah, who was sixteen years old, and made him king—Because it says, "the people took Uzziah," there are some indications that Uzziah's father was still alive but a captive in Samaria. If so, try to imagine what a difficult situation this young man was in.

- Have you ever been put into a situation for which you felt unprepared? If God is sovereign, are we ever truly unprepared?

2 After Amaziah the king rested with his ancestors, Uzziah rebuilt Eloth—This may signal the beginning of Uzziah's own reign. Eloth (or Elath) is important because it gave Judah access to sea trade and goods from India, Arabia, and Africa. The city had not been under Judah's control since the time of Solomon. It is a great compliment to Uzziah to connect him to Solomon.

- ♦ What determines whether or not a person is remembered by later generations? Consider this—how much do you know about your great-grandparents? Where did your information come from?

3 Uzziah was sixteen years old when he became king, and he reigned fifty-two years in Jerusalem.—The standard record of the kings. The name Uzziah means "the LORD is my strength," and Azariah means "the LORD helps." Notice how those ideas are realized in his life.

- ♦ We do not always place as much emphasis on the meaning of names. Do you think the meaning encouraged the young king? Now think about the name we've been given—Christian. Is that an encouragement? Why or why not?

4 He did what was right in the LORD's sight just as his father Amaziah had done.—As we've seen previously, notice how God remembers things versus how history remembers.

- ♦ Read Isaiah 43:25. What does it say about God's memory?

5 He sought God throughout the lifetime of Zechariah, the teacher of the fear of God. During the time that he sought the Lord, God gave him success—This Zechariah is not one we're familiar with. It was a popular name. At least thirty-four different people with the name are mentioned in Scripture.

This verse highlights two things we've seen before that lead to success and blessing.

1.

2.

Live the Message

It is impossible to know for certain, but perhaps Uzziah understood that his father's problems started when he rejected godly mentors and embraced the Edomite gods. Ruling a kingdom as a young man is a huge undertaking, and Uzziah leaned on Zechariah for guidance. We need to seek advice, as well. Think for a moment what new experiences are in front of you and think about what you've already experienced—getting married soon? Starting a family? Buying a house? Changing jobs? Raising teenagers? Sending kids to college? Becoming grandparents? Retiring? What questions do you have? Who could be a resource?

What wisdom have you gained? Who might benefit from it?

Text 2/3

2 Chronicles 26:6-15 (CSB)

6 Uzziah went out to wage war against the Philistines, and he tore down the wall of Gath, the wall of Jabneh, and the wall of Ashdod. Then he built cities in the vicinity of Ashdod and among the Philistines.

7 God helped him against the Philistines, the Arabs that live in Gurbaal, and the Meunites.

8 The Ammonites paid tribute to Uzziah, and his fame spread as far as the entrance of Egypt, for God made him very powerful.

9 Uzziah built towers in Jerusalem at the Corner Gate, the Valley Gate, and the corner buttress, and he fortified them.

10 Since he had many cattle both in the Judean foothills and the plain, he built towers in the desert and dug many wells. And since he was a lover of the soil, he had farmers and vinedressers in the hills and in the fertile lands.

11 Uzziah had an army equipped for combat that went out to war by division according to their assignments, as recorded by Jeiel the court secretary and Maaseiah the officer under the authority of Hananiah, one of the king's commanders.

12 The total number of family heads was 2,600 valiant warriors.

13 Under their authority was an army of 307,500 equipped for combat, a powerful force to help the king against the enemy.

14 Uzziah provided the entire army with shields, spears, helmets, armor, bows, and slingstones.

15 He made skillfully designed devices in Jerusalem to shoot arrows and catapult large stones for use on the towers and on the corners. So his fame spread even to distant places, for he was wondrously helped until he became strong.

Study the Text

FOCUS

FOCUS on the passage above. What FACTS are presented?

Are there any instructions to OBEY?

Do you see anything in the passage that reminds you of CHRIST?

Was there anything that was difficult to UNDERSTAND?

Are there any SINS to avoid?

Insights

6 Uzziah went out to wage war against the Philistines—The cities in this verse are all Philistine cities. You may have noticed Gath, the hometown of the giant Goliath. While we might pass over these details, they would have stirred the consciousness of the contemporary readers. These acts connected Uzziah with King David.

♦ Why might it be especially important in this history written for returning exiles to draw comparisons to David and Solomon?

8 The Ammonites paid tribute to Uzziah, and his fame spread as far as the entrance of Egypt, for God made him very powerful.—With these victories, Uzziah subdued enemies to the west, east, and south. (Only Israel to the north remained.)

♦ Review verses 5-8 and mark all the references to God. Why was Uzziah successful?

10 Since he had many cattle both in the Judean foothills and the plain, he built towers in the desert and dug many wells. And since he was a lover of the soil, he had farmers and vinedressers in the hills and in the fertile lands.—Again, these details are reminiscent of Solomon.

14 Uzziah provided the entire army with shields, spears, helmets, armor, bows, and slingstones.—As strange as it seems to us, until this point, soldiers in Judah supplied their own equipment. This was a radical change and indicated the importance Uzziah placed on his troops themselves.

♦ How do people respond to a leader they believe is personally invested in their success? Are you an invested leader? How do your people know that?

15 He made skillfully designed devices in Jerusalem to shoot arrows and catapult large stones for use on the towers and on the corners. So his fame spread even to distant places, for he was wondrously helped until he became strong.—These devices are thought to be something like an early version of a catapult-type thing.

♦ Circle the words that play off the meanings of Uzziah's name.

Live the Message

Consider Uzziah's list of accomplishments. Was he prosperous? How do you define prosperity? Where does prosperity come from?

Read 1 Corinthians 12:28-31 and 1 Corinthians 13:1-3. Now read Jeremiah 9:23—24. Does God value prosperity?

Do prosperity and its pursuit ever become sinful? Under what circumstances? Does the Western church adequately teach and admonish about prosperity?

Text 3/3

2 Chronicles 26:16-23 (CSB)

16 But when he became strong, he grew arrogant, and it led to his

own destruction. He acted unfaithfully against the Lord his God by going into the LORD's sanctuary to burn incense on the incense altar.

17 The priest Azariah, along with eighty brave priests of the Lord, went in after him.

18 They took their stand against King Uzziah and said, "Uzziah, you have no right to offer incense to the Lord—only the consecrated priests, the descendants of Aaron, have the right to offer incense. Leave the sanctuary, for you have acted unfaithfully! You will not receive honor from the Lord God."

19 Uzziah, with a firepan in his hand to offer incense, was enraged. But when he became enraged with the priests, in the presence of the priests in the LORD's temple beside the altar of incense, a skin disease broke out on his forehead.

20 Then Azariah the chief priest and all the priests turned to him and saw that he was diseased on his forehead. They rushed him out of there. He himself also hurried to get out because the Lord had afflicted him.

21 So King Uzziah was diseased to the time of his death. He lived in quarantine with a serious skin disease and was excluded from access to the LORD's temple, while his son Jotham was over the king's household governing the people of the land.

22 Now the prophet Isaiah son of Amoz wrote about the rest of the events of Uzziah's reign, from beginning to end.

23 Uzziah rested with his ancestors, and he was buried with his ancestors in the burial ground of the kings' cemetery, for they said, "He has a skin disease." His son Jotham became king in his place.

Study the Text

FOCUS

FOCUS on the passage above. What FACTS are presented?

Are there any instructions to OBEY?

Do you see anything in the passage that reminds you of CHRIST?

Was there anything that was difficult to UNDERSTAND?

Are there any SINS to avoid?

Insights

16 But when he became strong, he grew arrogant, and it led to his own destruction.—This is a very Jewish way to relay the account. We have a summary statement, and then the writer will give us some more details.

- ♦ In the last session, in 2 Chronicles 25:19, Amaziah displayed a level of arrogance as well. Why does dangerous pride follow success?

17 The priest Azariah, along with eighty brave priests of the Lord, went in after him.— Even though there were eighty priests, they are still called brave.

- ♦ How difficult is it to challenge wrongdoing by leaders? Is that why the priests are called brave? Read 1 Timothy 5:9. How does that safeguard relate to this situation?

18 Leave the sanctuary, for you have acted unfaithfully!—"Acted unfaithfully" is "transgressed," and it means Uzziah crossed a line. In Numbers 3:10 and 18:7, the Law clearly states the burning incense was a function reserved solely for the priests

- ♦ This moment is an opportunity for Uzziah to repent. His sin has been pointed out. His response will reveal his heart. We are no different. How do people respond when confronted with sin? How do you typically respond?

19 But when he became enraged with the priests . . . a skin disease broke out on his forehead.—After Uzziah rejects the opportunity to repent, judgment falls. The leprosy is a visible, physical manifestation of that judgment.

- ♦ Read Daniel 4:27-33. What similarities do you see between what happened to Nebuchadnezzar and what happened to Uzziah? Does that suggest God has a way of dealing with pride?

21 So King Uzziah was diseased to the time of his death. He lived in quarantine with a serious skin disease and was excluded from access to the LORD's temple—Leviticus 13-14 give the tedious details of how the king was now subject to the priests' authority.

- ♦ We've mentioned before that Chronicles was written for the generation returning to the land after Babylonian captivity. How do you think this failure of Uzziah would connect with people who had been "exiled" and "excommunicated" for their sin?

22 Now the prophet Isaiah son of Amoz wrote about the rest of the events of Uzziah's reign, from beginning to end.—This is Isaiah the prophet, and while he does mention Uzziah in his book of prophecy that we have in our Bible, the history/ biography mentioned here no longer exists.

23 Uzziah rested with his ancestors, and he was buried with his ancestors in the burial ground of the kings' cemetery, for they said,

"He has a skin disease."—Notice he was buried on the same parcel of ground but NOT with the other kings. His isolation continued beyond his life.

♦ Read Proverbs 1:7 and 12:15. Do those verses give any insight into Uzziah and his actions? In Proverbs, someone is a fool if they reject God. Does Uzziah fit that definition? How is he still considered a king who did what was right?

Live the Message

Read Genesis 3:1-13. Do you see any parallels between Adam and Eve and Uzziah?

Does this suggest that Uzziah's sin is perhaps more universal than it first appeared?

Read 1 John 2:16. How would you characterize Uzziah's sin? Does this verse suggest it was unique to him?

Finally, read 1 Corinthians 10:12-13. How do those verses apply to Uzziah and to your own life?

What happens when people with power and/or money seem to be above the law and do not get punished for their transgressions? How does Uzziah's life speak to that?

Uzziah's Legacy

In 1972, Richard Nixon won the presidential election by what was, at that time, the largest electoral margin in history, winning 520 of an available 538 electoral votes. Challenger George McGovern didn't even carry his home state of South Dakota but only carried the home state of his running mate, Sargent Shriver. It was a stunning victory.

But it was a victory that no one remembers because of what happened in the next two years when the Watergate break-in was revealed.

Even Shakespeare tells us through Marc Antony in his eulogy for Julius Caesar:

> The evil that men do lives after them; The good is oft interred with their bones;

Uzziah was a rock star. He was a king with tremendous gifts and remarkable accomplishments. He put the people in mind of their golden years under David and Solomon.

Now though, he is mostly known for his death:

> In the year that King Uzziah died, I saw the Lord seated on a high and lofty throne, and the hem of his robe filled the temple. Isaiah 6:1 (CSB)

And for his presumption in trying to take over the priest's job of burning incense.

His life is a warning. God's boundaries exist for a reason. It is the height of foolishness to overstep them.

Review the passage and your notes. What did you learn? How do those lessons speak to your life? Record them here. Also check pages 103-105.

Next Session

In the next session, we will finish our look at some of the good kings of Judah with a study of Uzziah's son, Jotham. There is less written of

Jotham than any of the others. He seems to have lived a quiet, almost nerdy life. Even so, we can learn from his example.

7

Jotham–The Quiet King

Prepare

Gather your study materials one more time as we get ready to dive into the study of the last king in our survey. If you're studying with a group, make sure everyone else is settled and has everything they need. This session is a bit shorter than the others but still has some important applications for us. As you pray and prepare for the study, consider the following questions.

♦ How much influence do leaders (any leaders, political, social, or otherwise) have over you? Is that a good or a bad thing?

♦ How much influence do you have on those around you? Would you want to have more influence?

Text 1/2

2 Kings 15:32-38 (NLT)

32 Jotham son of Uzziah began to rule over Judah in the second year of King Pekah's reign in Israel.

33 He was twenty-five years old when he became king, and he reigned in Jerusalem sixteen years. His mother was Jerusha, the daughter of Zadok.

34 Jotham did what was pleasing in the LORD's sight. He did everything his father, Uzziah, had done.

35 But he did not destroy the pagan shrines, and the people still

offered sacrifices and burned incense there. He rebuilt the upper gate of the Temple of the LORD.

36 The rest of the events in Jotham's reign and everything he did are recorded in The Book of the History of the Kings of Judah.

37 In those days the LORD began to send King Rezin of Aram and King Pekah of Israel to attack Judah.

38 When Jotham died, he was buried with his ancestors in the City of David. And his son Ahaz became the next king.

Study the Text

FOCUS

FOCUS on the passage above. What FACTS are presented?

Are there any instructions to OBEY?

Do you see anything in the passage that reminds you of CHRIST?

Was there anything that was difficult to UNDERSTAND?

Are there any SINS to avoid?

Insights

32 Jotham son of Uzziah began to rule over Judah in the second year of King Pekah's reign in Israel.—Historically, we know that Jotham's reign began in 750 BC. Recall that he has already spent about ten years running the country while his father was in seclusion. He is extremely well-prepared for his task.

- ♦ We see several examples in Scripture of people who did a kind of internship before taking on greater responsibilities. Think of the Apostles and Timothy, Paul's protégé, for example. Would young ministers and would churches benefit from this type of internship? If so, why do you suppose more churches don't use this model?

33 His mother was Jerusha, the daughter of Zadok.—Jerusha came from a prominent priestly family. It is unknown but undeniable that she and her extended family had an influence on her son.

- ♦ You may have heard the adage, "The hand that rocks the cradle rules the world." Is that true?

34 He did everything his father, Uzziah, had done.—The writer doesn't give us many more details.

- ♦ Take a moment and look back at the first parts of the study on Uzziah. Broadly speaking, what were his accomplishments?

35 But he did not destroy the pagan shrines, and the people still offered sacrifices and burned incense there.—The writers of Scripture never shy away from reality. No sugarcoating here.

List the two shortcomings:

1.

2.

- ♦ How are these two related?

37 In those days the LORD began to send King Rezin of Aram and King Pekah of Israel to attack Judah.—This coalition of Israel and Syria would continue to be an issue for Judah until the Assyrians destroy them both.

♦ Note who is behind the attacks. Based on our previous sessions, what conclusions can you draw about Jotham's reign in his later years?

Live the Message

Isaiah prophesied during the reign of Jotham. Read Isaiah 1:16-20. This was specifically directed at Judah and Jerusalem. Are there any similarities with our culture?

We have no way to know whether Jotham was a popular king, only that he was a godly one. How difficult is it to remain steadfastly obedient to God in a culture that you are the minority?

Is it easier or more difficult for leaders to remain steadfast?

Text 2/2

2 Chronicles 27:1-9 (NLT)

1 Jotham was twenty-five years old when he became king, and he

reigned in Jerusalem sixteen years. His mother was Jerusha, the daughter of Zadok.

2 Jotham did what was pleasing in the LORD's sight. He did everything his father, Uzziah, had done, except that Jotham did not sin by entering the Temple of the LORD. But the people continued in their corrupt ways.

3 Jotham rebuilt the upper gate of the Temple of the LORD. He also did extensive rebuilding on the wall at the hill of Ophel.

4 He built towns in the hill country of Judah and constructed fortresses and towers in the wooded areas.

5 Jotham went to war against the Ammonites and conquered them. Over the next three years he received from them an annual tribute of 7,500 pounds of silver, 50,000 bushels of wheat, and 50,000 bushels of barley.

6 King Jotham became powerful because he was careful to live in obedience to the LORD his God.

7 The rest of the events of Jotham's reign, including all his wars and other activities, are recorded in The Book of the Kings of Israel and Judah.

8 He was twenty-five years old when he became king, and he reigned in Jerusalem sixteen years.

9 When Jotham died, he was buried in the City of David. And his son Ahaz became the next king.

Study the Text

FOCUS

FOCUS on the passage above. What FACTS are presented?

Are there any instructions to OBEY?

Do you see anything in the passage that reminds you of CHRIST?

Was there anything that was difficult to UNDERSTAND?

Are there any SINS to avoid?

Insights

2 He did everything his father, Uzziah, had done, except that Jotham did not sin by entering the Temple of the LORD.—No matter what else you may say about Jotham, he wasn't presumptuous. He was wise enough to learn from his father's sin.

♦ Can you think of someone's sin that made an impression on you? How effective are cautionary tales?

2 But the people continued in their corrupt ways.—The people are still held accountable for their sins. They don't get credit for the king's obedience.

♦ Recall 2 Kings 15:35 and the things Jotham left undone. Consider this in light of his steadfast obedience to God.

3-4 Jotham rebuilt the upper gate of the Temple of the LORD. He also did extensive rebuilding on the wall at the hill of Ophel. He built towns in the hill country of Judah and constructed fortresses and towers in the wooded areas.

List four of Jotham's building projects.

1.

2.

3.

4.

♦ What were building projects usually indicators of?

5 Jotham went to war against the Ammonites and conquered them. Over the next three years he received from them an annual tribute of 7,500 pounds of silver—Jotham reestablished the tribute payments from Ammon that had begun after his father's military victory.

6 King Jotham became powerful because he was careful to live in obedience to the LORD his God.—This could be the summary statement of the kings.

♦ In the original language, it says Jotham "caused his ways to be rightly ordered." Read 1 Samuel 7:3 and Psalm119:5-6. Does godliness just happen?

Live the Message

In 2 Chronicles 27:4-5, Jotham expends tremendous effort and resources to protect his kingdom from attack. Do we put a similar effort into protecting ourselves and our families from spiritual attack?

Read 2 Corinthians 10:4-5 and Romans 12:1-2. What is the battlefield for these attacks?

What influences what you think?

How do you determine if these are good influences or bad influences?

Jotham's Legacy

Jotham was a king with no moral courage. Moral conviction, yes. Moral discipline, yes. But courage, or will to act, no. He had the authority to eradicate idolatry in his kingdom and he did not.

His reign demonstrates the bankruptcy of the idea that we should not confront sin. Many hold to the idea that we simply need to live a godly life. If we are good, people will notice and want to imitate us. 2 Chronicles 27:2 tells us the "people continued in their corrupt ways."

Some might argue that people are free to live their own lives. We can't make them change. It is true we cannot exercise authoritarian power over others, but neither can we operate in a sanctified bubble, doing our thing while ungodliness continues to advance.

Jotham challenges us not to be passive but active. In Matthew 16:18, Jesus says the gates of hell will not prevail against His church. Think about that for a moment. A gate never attacked anyone. It is the church on the attack while hell is trying to defend itself. That's quite a different picture, isn't it?

The New Testament commands to the church are active. Go. Preach. Baptize. Teach. Don't sit back and wait for it to happen.

Review the passage and your notes. What did you learn? How do those lessons speak to your life? Record them here. Also check pages 103-105.

Next up, we'll wrap up our study.

8

Wrap-up—The Kings' Legacy

Here we are at the end of our survey of the good kings of Judah. Hopefully, you've been introduced to some people you may not have known and been challenged in your thinking.

This study has shown us that legacy is not destiny. Some of these good kings had wicked, idolatrous parents.

In the same way, some of these godly kings had sons and heirs who completely rejected their faith.

A couple of hundred years after these kings, the Babylonians came and carried the upper and middle classes into captivity in Babylon while the poorest people were left in the land to try to survive. Ezekiel the prophet was one of those carried away in 597 BC. He writes:

> 19 "Yet you say, 'Why should not the son suffer for the iniquity of the father?' When the son has done what is just and right, and has been careful to observe all my statutes, he shall surely live.
>
> 20 The soul who sins shall die. The son shall not suffer for the iniquity of the father, nor the father suffer for the iniquity of the son. The righteousness of the righteous shall be upon himself, and the wickedness of the wicked shall be upon himself.
>
> [. . .]
>
> 30 "Therefore I will judge you, O house of Israel, every one according to his ways, declares the Lord GOD. Repent and turn from all your transgressions, lest iniquity be your ruin.
>
> 31 Cast away from you all the transgressions that you have committed, and make yourselves a new heart and a new spirit! Why will you die, O house of Israel?
>
> 32 For I have no pleasure in the death of anyone, declares the Lord GOD; so turn, and live."
>
> **Ezekiel 18:19-20, 30-32 (ESV)**

Based on what Ezekiel wrote, how does God judge people—individually or corporately?

Is there evidence of this in the lives of the kings we studied?

Way back in the introduction, we looked at a verse in Romans:

> For whatever was written in former days was written for our instruction, that through endurance and through the encouragement of the Scriptures we might have hope. Romans 15:4

All of these things were written and preserved to teach us and to encourage us. Record some of the things you learned about God and His ways.

Record some things you learned about people and human nature.

Record what you learned about yourself.

What do you want your legacy to be? Here is a type of record we saw for the kings. What would you enter for it?

_____

(Your name)

became a believer in Christ at age _____ and has been a believer

for _____ years, and did what was _____ in the

eyes of the Lord.

(List some things you've done in obedience to God)

How do you want to be remembered?

Report Card

Give Each King a Letter Grade

Choose your grading criteria and give each of the kings we studied a letter grade A through F. Feel free to add + or —.

Asa

Jehoshaphat

Joash

Amaziah

Uzziah

Jotham

Things to Imitate

What good traits or acts from the kings are worth imitating?

Asa

Jehoshaphat

Joash

Amaziah

Uzziah

Jotham

Things to Avoid

What questionable traits or acts from the kings should be avoided?

Asa

Jehoshaphat

Joash

Amaziah

Uzziah

Jotham

Now What?

God never intends for the study of Scripture to simply be an opportunity to acquire knowledge. He means for the Word to change us, transform us to be more like Christ.

You've done great work investing your time and energy in this study. God always blesses that kind of investment. But for the investment in this study to really pay spiritual dividends, you can just relegate it to a shelf or a drawer and move on.

What will be different in your walk with Christ because of what you learned?

What will you strengthen, continue to do, or do more of?

Also by Paula Wiseman

Fiction
The Covenant of Trust Series
Contingency
Indemnity
Precedent
Sanction

The Foundations Series
Razed
Refined
Resolute

The Encounters Series
Touched
Embraced
Undone

Devotional
56 Tips to Help You Get the Most Out of Every Book in the Bible
The Race Set Before Us
Build the Altar

Visit www.paulawiseman.com

www.ingramcontent.com/pod-product-compliance
Lightning Source LLC
Chambersburg PA
CBHW030110070426
42448CB00036B/594